The Egyptian Tarot

A WAY OF INITIATION

by

BERND A. MERTZ

Translated by

Michael F. Lacey

with newly designed cards
for the Major Arcana by

Kamilla Szij

Editing and book design by

Rick Leaman

AuthorHouse™ UK Ltd.
500 Avebury Boulevard
Central Milton Keynes, MK9 2BE
www.authorhouse.co.uk
Phone: 08001974150

First published by AuthorHouse 05/10/2011

ISBN: 978-1-4567-7700-5

Author

Bernd A. Mertz was born in Berlin on 10th July 1924, spending the war and post-war years there, where he worked as an author for theatre, radio and television. He rapidly developed an intensive interest in psychology and esotericism. First of all as a hobby, then professionally, he wrote over a period of thirty years some fifty books about astrology, tarot, numerology etc. He was fascinated by the inner experiences, insights and transformations which he found in these fields. He held talks, gave courses, and is considered one of the most important astrologers of our times.

Through his journeys to Egypt a deep relationship evolved towards the tarot and its mystic picture language which he interpreted for us comprehensibly and memorably.

Kamilla Szij designed the symbol figures convincingly to create a modern view of the images.

Numerous books by Bernd A. Mertz have been translated into the languages of many countries: for instance the Netherlands, Denmark, Norway, Spain, Poland, Hungary, the Czech Republic, Slovakia, Russia, Brazil.

For his readers Bernd A. Mertz always provided explanations and interpretations for the pictures in clear and passionate words. What they say is intended to move the soul and our feelings. They can be a key for problems of our times so that we are able to find help and solutions.

Christiane Mertz,
Frankfurt am Main, 2010

Translator

Michael F. Lacey, born in Essex UK, has acted as translator for a number of books and has published poetry and novels in his own right under the pen name of Francis Michaels (francismichaels.com). He graduated in Germanic and Slavonic languages and literature and has worked in adult education as a business consultant, trainer and coach based in Germany for many years. This book is a result of his astrological and esoteric interests which led him to a group co-operating still fifteen years after the death of Bernd A. Mertz who initiated it.

Editor

Rick Leaman, born in Maine USA, is a graduate of the University of Pennsylvania with degrees in Anthropology and Communications. He lived many years in Vienna, Austria working as a communications consultant and delegate to the United Nations. His first book, East-West Guide, was a post-Cold War resource for commercial cooperation between eastern Europe and the west. This book is a natural result of his career interest in iconography as a communication aid to insight, personal awareness and understanding.

CONTENTS

Why This Book?

P aris two hundred years ago - anno 1781. One question that Court de Gébelin asked in his *work "Monde Primitif" (Primitive World) attracted great attention in Parisian esoteric circles which were shooting out of the dark like mushrooms. Gébelin asked in a rather mysterious and long-winded manner:

'Imagine the surprise that would occur today if one were, say, to announce that a work of the ancient Egyptians still exists, one of their books that had escaped the flames which devoured their superb libraries, and which contains their purest tenets on subjects of interest; everyone would, undoubtedly, hasten to become familiar with such an exceptional book...

Would I also not increase your surprise if I asserted that this book is very widespread in many parts of Europe, that for a number of centuries it has not been lost but has been so to speak in the hands of everyone. Would it not be most astonishing of all, if one gave assurances that no one ever suspected that it was Egyptian; that those who possessed it did not realize it, that hardly anyone has ever sought to decipher a page of it; that the fruit of an extraordinary wisdom is regarded as a heap of extravagant figures which have no intrinsic meaning?'

This is the question to which Gébelin himself provided the following answer:

'It is nonetheless a fact: this Egyptian book, the only survivor of their superb libraries, exists in our day - after all the treasures and all the knowledge of the Egyptian libraries have been lost: it has even become so popular that no sage has deigned to occupy himself with it; nobody has ever suspected its illustrious origin; no-one apart from us.'

And then, at another point:

'...in a word, it's all about the game of Tarot!'

We would like to decipher this ancient book and issue a new edition of the cards, adapted for our times.

The origin of the Tarot cannot be proved with one hundred percent certainty. Whoever has been in the temples or tombs of the ancient Egyptians, however, will have discovered the astonishing correspondence of numerous images and artistic depictions - as regards the basic motifs - with those of the twenty-two picture 'laws' of the Tarot's Major Arcana. They will know that the ancient temple statements still have validity today because they reflect prehistoric stages of development and awareness. In addition to this, it is also certain that the priests taught the seekers and those not yet initiated by means of these pictorial motifs, thus guiding them into the secrets of arcane knowledge.

Esoteric knowledge at that time used to be at the core of every religion-oriented study which pursued the objective of making the sense of life clear and understandable, so that life could be meaningfully lived out. The twenty-two pictorial motifs of the Major Arcana contain the stages of awareness and development of an individual life; they represent the milestones on the Way which the uninitiated took in order to become adepts in ancient wisdom, to achieve initiation.

In doing so it was less mental logic which played the main role, although this was also trained and scientific-oriented thinking also existed then, but rather the fact of grasping everything with an inner knowledge which became a conviction (instead of vice versa). Thus at the initiation it was less a matter of a logic aligned to the understanding, able to be grasped by everyone, than of an inner understanding of the knowledge of the human soul and of being embedded in a great order of the cosmos.

Therefore, it seems a natural consequence that the ancient Egyptian Tarot - even if it is newly interpreted here and artistically recreated - is not misused for some banal fortune-telling. The work will show that the far greater value of these cards lies in the encounter with oneself, in order to accommodate oneself thus to the esoteric world. For this reason the accompanying Tarot set only consists of the twenty-two cards of the Major Arcana.

The Minor Arcana of the four card suits is completely missing; these anyway count more as picture and number cards, without having all that much significance in their communication value. It is not without reason that the familiar card games have developed from these, with which one can play for 'money or other rewards' and which would certainly have little to do with esoteric experience.

The cards of the Major Arcana consist of twenty-one pictures plus the card called 'The Initiate' which bears the number zero and twenty-two as its indicator, both being numbers which lie outside the two holy numbers of three and seven, that make up twenty-one when multiplied. One might in addition conclude that before the one and after the twenty-one everything can be considered 'foolish' - or alternatively - uninitiated.

The card named 'The Fool', which is called 'The Initiate' in the accompanying Tarot, leads us onto the Way of initiation and, on concluding this Way, onto a further path which should help us in achieving a further level in our development. When it concerns the interpretation and significance of this card, it becomes evident that it is precisely the ancient Egyptian wisdom which we are facing when we are making our own life experience. In such moments it becomes clear how timeless these pictures are, which means that the cards are not so much modern as exceptionally appropriate for our time.

The Egyptian goddess of death, Serket symbol of card thirteen - says at one point in ancient Egyptian myths: '*I have seen Yesterday - I know Tomorrow*'

This can be applied here to the Tarot, since it communicates the awareness and wisdom of the past in order to be equipped for today and tomorrow.

This finds its very special expression in the three types of spread: in the 'Minor Egyptian guiding star' for daily tasks and the 'Major Egyptian guiding star' as the motto for life goals which are relevant at the present time. One can meet one's shadow in the spread 'The Ways of Thoth' which makes each person aware that no-one can and may only seek out the sunny side of life in any issue.

(*Footnote: Monde primitif, analysé et comparé avec le monde moderne [The Primitive World, Analyzed and Compared to the Modern World] (volume 8), which includes his famous essay on Tarot.)

INSIGHT

AND

KNOWLEDGE

IN

ANCIENT

EGYPT

One statement should be made at the start so that we take in the pictures of the ancient Egyptian Tarot correctly: all the paintings in the temples and tombs which we refer to in the Major Arcana are to be imagined as magically animated. This magic animation explains the nature of the impact which these motifs have had until the present. Magic itself, and everything that was magic, always played a significant role in the Egyptian world and in its history, and was later transformed into mysticism. How old Egyptian culture is can be measured by the fact that the oldest skeletons excavated were 60,000 to 80,000 years old, as old as the Neanderthals. However, at that time in Egypt there was already a highly developed culture, which can be seen in the manner of burials. Very early the dead were consigned to eternal rest in cemeteries or locations with tombs outside the settlements. When doing so, magic figures (amulets), jewelry and other accompanying objects were placed alongside. The dead were buried in a squatting position, an indication of the idea that they found themselves from then onwards on a great journey.

Fear of the demons of death hardly existed, for with the enhancement of magic to mysticism a kind of conversion into the divine took place with demons that people sought to integrate into the world of the gods. The depictive works which were also created for this purpose were called "life makers" by the Egyptians, by the way, and even the sculptors were called by this name, as well. These depictive works and statues had in the first instance to incorporate the sense of being containers for the vital power of the dead, which is especially important for the interpretation of the Tarot cards, as the Egyptians believed they could breathe the life force and transfer the breath of life into the dead by means of magic rites.

From this it is also understandable that the card "The Initiate" (otherwise usually called the "Fool") is placed in sequence both before and after the cards of the Major Arcana as number 0 and XXII. It stands at the beginning and at the end, in which a new beginning is already born. A fact, which has been mostly overlooked till now, points very significantly to the Egyptian origin of the Tarot: card II, "The Empress" or "The Pharaoh Queen" comes before card IV "The Emperor" or "The Pharaoh King". It is only from the history of the Egyptian ruling houses that one can understand why the female Pharaoh comes to be placed before the male Pharaoh. Doubtless already originating from the time of the matriarchy, the woman had precedence over the man, above all as regards the right of succeeding to the throne as Pharaoh, especially in the third and fourth dynasties; and this principle permeates the whole of ancient Egyptian history.

These laws passed down through time also meant, as a consequence, that marriages between brothers and sisters were celebrated when it was a question of legitimizing claims to the throne through marriage to a princess. It should not be ignored in such cases that the pharaohs also understood themselves as divine rulers, who therefore ruled on earth only as representatives of the godhead. Thus the female pharaohs were perceived as the direct representatives of Isis, which is expressed in card III.

So if it depended on the king's daughter who would become pharaoh, if she did not grasp the scepter herself, it is only logical that the female pharaoh (Empress) comes before the male pharaoh (Emperor). However, female pharaohs themselves also took on the leadership of the state with very considerable skills. The most well-known example for this is (Queen) Pharaoh Hathespsut. Her almost 30 meter high obelisk can still be admired today in Karnak.

All this speaks for the fact that the motifs of Tarot are very ancient, even if most of the games which are found on the market today can be described as products of their times, reflecting the trends and fashion of their particular epoch of origin. It seems to be all the more important, therefore, to get involved with the original pictures of Tarot again in order to fathom their original significance.

Ancient Egyptian culture has also without any doubt decisively shaped our own western culture, as the great Greek historian, Herodotus, stated when he informed us with the first reports from and about Egypt. Herodotus wrote among other things that the Egyptians were the first to have discovered the year (which meant the solar year, in any case providing the basis for our astrology). The Egyptians furthermore divided - according to Herodotus - the year into twelve months, which is why they were also aware of twelve main gods, whom the Greeks then took over from them.

In Egypt the first altars were also erected to the gods and later temples which were decorated with the images of the divine. Herodotus further reported that almost all the names of the gods taken over by the Greeks and later by the Romans were of Egyptian origin.

How holy the temples were to the Egyptians can be concluded from the fact that no-one was allowed to copulate there, just as it was also taboo to enter a temple unwashed after coitus. These examples already demonstrate how very precisely the Egyptian priests considered the supervision and maintenance of their religious customs. These were the same priests who supervised the initiation ceremonies with all strictness, for only those who had proved themselves worthy were actually initiated. Thus even the pre-examinations were very important; only after they had been passed was it possible to begin the schooling for initiation.

There were so many aspirants that a strict selection was possible. Initiation counted as a special distinction, but also as an obligation to serve the gods with the knowledge acquired and thus serve human beings too. Initiation imparted also the awareness that the human soul was immortal. Indeed this belief was widely spread among all the Egyptian peoples (Egypt consisted of several tribal peoples) but the initiated did not only believe in a further life, they really knew about it, even if that seems alien to today's scientific thought.

The basis of knowledge and teaching of every initiation was the Book of Thoth. Thoth was the god of time, the god of the sciences, and most of his characteristics were later transferred to the Greek god, Chronos, or to the Roman god, Saturn. Thoth, who had nothing to do with Hermes Trismegistus, the thrice mighty, was often depicted with an ibis head, sometimes also with the head of a baboon. The stork-like Ibis announced a decisive time-change, since he came with the Nile floods which allowed a time of fertility to begin.

The book of Thoth was said to have originally consisted only of the 22 pictures of the Major Arcana; this cannot be proved, however. It is more probable that these 22 pictures were indeed contained in the book of wisdom, at least as basic motifs, but that there was still more content hidden in this book. There are indications, however, that future adepts (initiates) grappled with these holy images during their initiation phase in school and temple, which included also meditations about the content of the images.

The goal of these meditations was that the understanding or rational mind should absorb and grasp as a store of knowledge what the soul already knew. Today a similar approach is used by psychologists or psychoanalysts who want to transfer the knowledge of the soul or whatever is stored in the sub-conscious, into the conscious mind. Here it is, however, more a matter of the personal memories of the soul, whereas in ancient Egypt there was an inherited (genetic) memory, which also contained the belief in the re-materialization of the body. This conviction was held by the Egyptian religion and provided the occasion for the embalming of the dead bodies, for which the journey into the other world could thus be facilitated. We know today that the mummies stayed on the Earth and are without life, that there is no such thing as a re-materialization of the body in the sense of a resurrection, but that the further existence takes place on the astral level, from which the soul comes and to which it returns.

The form and shape are not of significance then; it is the content, at the level of mind, that we must dedicate our efforts to.

The Egyptian priests had doubtless been the first to realize that the gods were by no means prepared to reveal their total knowledge to humans without any reciprocation, i.e. without any real effort. They also realized that there was far more knowledge than the average person was able to imagine. Nowadays we quote in this sense: "There are more things in heaven and earth, Horatio, than are dreamt of in our philosophy."

This knowledge about more things is also to be found in the 22 cards of the Major Arcana, indeed one might say that these 22 pictorial motifs contain in partly encrypted symbols the whole knowledge which can be revealed to mankind, even if this knowledge does not depict divine knowledge per se. But whoever has assimilated, grasped and has really understood these symbols, knows more than the average person; she/he is on the way to become an adept, i.e. an initiate, a disciple.

Unfortunately most fashionable Tarot games, even those from the late Middle Ages, contain only superficial symbols which are not really understood. Many Tarot packs are just to be treated as games, as they only show superficial images whose sense, nature and content have got completely lost. The Tarot presented here is indeed newly created but is based on the most ancient Egyptian motifs with which we can reproduce a Way of Initiation which applies to our times. It is about the deep mystery of the Book of Thoth. Each Tarot card stands for a developmental step which we can but are not obliged to find reflected in human beings. Each card represents a potential stage of insight through which we are able to get near or at least nearer to the meaning of life.

Here it seems important that not every human development in insight becomes apparent in the order corresponding to the numbering and thus the sequence of the cards. In life the cards are shuffled; we often jump from one experience level to the next but one. Or we even experience larger leaps - forwards and also backwards. This is determined by each person's basic understanding of life, by impressions from upbringing and education, by processes of destiny.

However, in each jump from one card to the other a secret sense is hidden which we must discover. The knowledge of this sense can lead us to our center, from which the whole power and strength can be drawn which is available to each of us. It concerns the center: between body and mind on the one side and the soul on the other. If this center has been found, we experience destiny as the processual flow of a great, because divine, dimension.

THE SOUL IN EGYPTIAN MYTH

1 n ancient Egypt the spiritual always had a superior significance. In the 'sacred' literature we repeatedly meet three terms for the soul, namely Ka, Ba and Ach. These terms do not stand alongside each other; it is rather that they can hardly be distinguished from each other, since their meanings overlap or blend with each other. Thus individually they can only be explained in an incomplete fashion. Nevertheless we will try to do this here:

The energies living, procreating and nurturing in human beings, which emerge with the body in the same form - indeed even before birth - are termed Ka. Thus Ka represents the creative god-head operating in each human being, the constant flow of vitality; therefore, 'going to Ka' also means dying. Ka is then whatever lives, whether we feel/sense the life or not. After the dead are judged (card VIII) Ka would fly back into the shell of the body – if the court had not condemned the heart and thrown it to Ammut – in order to resuscitate the body, which means to make a re-embodiment possible.

Ba is the psyche which separates itself from the body after death and rises up to heaven. This is comparable with the last breath in the karma process with which the soul leaves the body. It has entered the body with the first breath in order during a lifetime to gain the experience which it is intended to have on the way to Nirvana, even if this is only one step after another. After departing from the corpse Ba can act according to its own judgement; only Osiris can get Ba to re-unite with the body in order then to expire for ever through a second death.

Ach represents the immortal power that can transfigure humans and gods, but that is also connected to demons, which were perceived as beings or apparitions between gods and men.

The notions behind Ren, Ab, Khat and Khaibit were also important for the ancient Egyptians' ideas about belief. Ren was the term for the name by which the human being first received his value. Ab stood for the heart which filled the body (Khat) with life but which had to grapple with Khaibit, the shadow. All these existential energies make up the human being in his completeness and share in determining his fate.

This variety is reflected in the whole of the ancient Egyptians' life and is naturally also expressed in the Tarot motifs.

Additionally they also shared a conviction that everything - and thus also humans too - were interconnected in the cosmos, a fact which was particularly evident in the architecture of the temples. Every temple was supposed to symbolize the cosmos. Thus the columns of plants (Papyrus or Lotus) represented the primordial swamp, the ceiling the primal vault of heaven (i.e. the one which is no longer visible), the space located high up for the cult image symbolized the very first hill. The main alignment of the temple was also marked by the obelisk in front of the entrance. At the summer solstice the sun stood exactly over the highest point of the temple in the early morning. The centre point of every holy place was the image of the deity which mostly stood in the darkest room, furthest from the entrance, and was made either out of stone or some precious metal.

These gods were addressed by those praying with a conviction that divine beings were among them in the world, though the statues themselves were never perceived as gods.

The statue was only a receptacle into which the deity could enter, should she/he wish to temporarily occupy the temple. This idea was later taken over by the astrologers who never equated the planets with the corresponding deities but always spoke of the planet of the particular god. So the planet Saturn was only the symbol of the Saturn principle and the powers and tasks allocated to him. Astrology played an important role in ancient Egypt, which is expressed most visibly in the image of the death goddess Serket, since she wears the scorpion on her head as an attribute and as an adornment.

The Egyptians were aware of the principle of the good and bad days, which was not to be understood in the banal sense but referred rather to the light and dark sides of a matter. This knowledge about the true process of life committed people to a community in which the initiated had taken the leadership. Astrologers were respected, they counted as adepts and were mostly priests in their practical function. They exercised their office on the roofs of the holy places, i.e. the temples, which speaks for their acceptance and their significance.

Only the "Highest Adepts" were allowed to enter the room in which the image of the cult stood. Their task was to carry out rituals there such as the daily opening of the shrine, the morning cleansing for the statue, which was concluded with the burning of incense, the changing of garments of the statue, the closing of the shrine in the evening.

It was finally due to the influence of the astrologers that an awareness spread that only the sun god Ra, who was symbolized by the regular course of the sun, guaranteed the overall structure of the world.

Representing the sun god Ra, his daughter Ma'at watched over divine justice on earth. However, this did not relate to any worldly affairs but only had an impact in the final verdict at the judgement of the dead.

Ma'at, the symbol of justice, was once again embodied by Pharaoh, who felt himself to be the representative of the deity, a fact that was accepted by the people (though less so by the priests). No wonder the statues of the pharaohs often bore such similarity to the gods.

The name pharaoh comes from the Bible and was derived from the Egyptian Per-aa, which means roughly great house or mansion. The effigy of the ruler, later of the leading persons of the country, was always perceived as being very important because it depicted the value of a life as being far beyond death.

The Egyptian name for a copy from life is Schesep-Anch (Living Statue). The Greek word sphinx originated from this. The sphinx in male or female form was often created with the body of a lion and the face of a person, the face mostly showing similarities to a pharaoh. When considering the spiritual world of the Egyptians we must always bear in mind that our current logic of how to understand things would not only appear alien to the Egyptians but even incomprehensible. The Egyptians did not live in a world of abstract concepts but in a world of pictures just as they considered being integrated in the cosmos as a pictorial concept as well. Thus initiation was also sought and found through images.

THE WAYS TO INITIATION

There are seven ways in all:

.... *The Way of the Initiate*

.... *The Way of the Magician*

.... *The Way of the High Priestess*

.... *The Way of Osiris*

.... *The Way of Isis*

.... *The Way of Horus*

.... *The Ways of Thoth*

The last of these ways already provides a type of spread in which every person is able to recognize their individual light side and the shadow belonging to it. The first six ways are then paths of learning, whereas the last way, the type of spread used, is revealed as a primary experience.

In the whole field of esotericism there is a principle which states that everything has its complement within itself. Thus the centre includes above and below, left and right. Life knows the past and the future; the soul knows both life and death; the beginning knows the end and the end the beginning. Day needs night and night requires day; evil needs the good and vice versa. Understanding esotericism begins by our not only realizing the opposite, which lies in all things, but also by truly acknowledging this: thus the odd number belongs to the even number, to pro-creation belongs conception. Thus too the most holy numbers from one to nine, which are to lead us to initiation, are perceived as uninitiated numbers. The single-figure numbers, neverthe-less, still retain the unholy within themselves since they have not yet found their complement.

The Egyptians never believed in one God alone, except during Achenaton's era, which in relation to the whole period of ancient Egyptian history represents only the passing of a minute. Hardly had Achenaton passed away than the Egyptians returned under the leadership of their priests to their world of multiple gods. The 'Revolutionary' Achenaton (Amenophis IV) ruled for only 16 years (1378-1362 BCE). He was the first king to break with traditional ideas about belief and to introduce monotheism as a state religion. Achenaton substituted the old gods by the one God, Aton. After his death, however, the whole of Egypt returned to the old religious conceptions and thereby also to the magic rites experienced as wise and good. Achenaton's idea of a belief system, as an artificially created view, was neither accepted by the priesthood, nor by adepts, let alone by the people.

The Egyptians held the view that everything - even the highest godhead - had an opposite pole, needed an adversary. Basically we find this conviction again later in the Western myths of the Greeks and Romans, just as we do in the religions which followed, including Christianity, where Lucifer transforms into the devil, who raises his torch (of rebellion) against the one cre-ative God. The Egyptians were not yet aware of any concept 'Devil', not even 'Typhon', who later became familiar in the Greek myths. The evil counterpart was inconceivable, evil living as it did in every God, as in every human being. They preferred to call it demon which is why the card of the Devil (XV) in our Egyptian Tarot also bears the name of 'Demon'.

The sun has to descend into the underworld daily and be guided through it. Furthermore the sun god Ra (also known as Re) emerges in connection with many other gods, as if to document that linkage is first of all essential: a dualistic approach which leads to the goal. In this sense the many animal gods can be understood, since Horus is depicted with a falcon's head, Hathor with the head of a cow and Thoth with the head of an ibis or a baboon, while the death goddess Serket bears the scorpion on her head full of pride.

Less familiar gods included Taweret, whose hippo head filled people both with fear and trust, or the ram god Khnum, whose golden horns often gleamed far into the surrounding land. The cat god, Bastet, as well as the lion goddess, Sekhmet, were depicted with the heads of these animals in order to record that the sacred resided in animals as does the animal in human beings.

However, Ra always represented the greatest (though not the highest) divinity, which is why others allied themselves with him, a fact which found expression in the many local gods. Even Achenaton, who only wanted to permit one god to be recognized, named his god Aton, the lord of life, the creator and protector of the world, Ra-Horakhty. In this connection we can read:

"... who rejoiceth on the horizon in his name as the light that is in the sun."

It was impossible to establish this belief within one and a half decades, for it is the soul that must believe - not the rational mind. A contrasting example is familiar to us from Christianity where the worship of the Virgin was forbidden but still continued to survive among ordinary people until the Catholic curia was forced to permit the worship of Maria. Whatever lives in the soul is the true knowledge, not whatever haunts the head. The images of the ancient Egyptian Major Arcana in the tarot are similarly based on ancient spiritual experience.

Only the soul itself has experienced this in just such a way: namely that dualism, that the complementary, that the starting point and the destination, in fact that everything lies within us. Thus divine pairs rule, such as Sun and Moon and later, for instance, Venus and Mars or Jupiter and Saturn, However, all of this awareness was already true for the time prior to the creation of order in this world, namely for the time when all of life seems to have emerged from the ancient ocean.

This was also an image derived from what could be experienced annually along the Nile. For after the flooding of the Nile, which inundated whole stretches of land under mud and water, everyone was able to observe how islands were born out of the floods. That's how the Egyptians imagined the creation of the earth. For, whoever experienced this scene for the first time with a naive and impressionable soul, remembered it as an unforgettable memory buried deep inside the soul.

There were eight gods - 'ogdoad' (eight being the number of infinity), i.e. four pairs of gods, who ruled as symbols of the once chaotic elements. The first pair of gods were called Nun and Naunet. They personified the ancient ocean and were depicted as snake or frog-shaped (as were most divinities still categorized as chaotic). The second pair were named Huh and Hauhet symbolizing infinite space, while the third pair from this epoch, Kuk and Kauket, stood for ancient darkness, for eternal gloom. The last pair of gods from this era of the creation of the world out of Chaos were called Amun and Amaunet representing the empty nothingness of infinity. It was then incidentally Amun, too, whom they called the Hidden One and who had drawn all these divinities together in order to create an order for this world according to his plan of creation. In the present time these four pairs of gods remind us somewhat of the four elements which for the Greeks represented the foundation of all life and which also became the basis of astronomy.

It was therefore always self-evident for 'initiated' Egyptians that only a pair of gods , i.e. two divinities, were able to create and initiate something new. This deeply-rooted acceptance of complementarity led to a perfection of human thinking which today, in our epoch of individualism, the cult of self-realization, we can hardly imagine, let alone relate to.

This pair-experience, as the core of all inner maturity, we can experience in the spread: 'The Ways of Thoth', since here it is a question in the first instance of accepting one's shadow. In this way we experience a more profound dimension of the Book of Thoth than other tarots really permit. This may guide us to new thinking or indeed to a new level of maturity (also to a more deeply experienced meditation).

For practical work with the cards it means that we always have to imagine a zero in front of the cards with the numbers I to IX (1 to 9). The zero card represents the Initiate, so all cards with single-figure numbers are to be linked to the symbol of the Initiate. From card X to XIX (10 to 19) there is always an involvement of the Magician, and with XX to XXI (20 to 21) the High Priestess. Particularly the cards in which the zero appears as the second figure, cards X (10) and XX (20), have special significance in showing a new way: one which we can also categorize as a new level of development. Only now can we grasp to some degree the magic of the ancient Egyptians which was always experienced as being of great potency.

Naturally the priests in Egypt were already familiar with the other version of magic which we nowadays call black magic. What was meant at that time was that any abuse of magic (today described as black) directed against religion, that is against the gods, was to be scrutinized and rejected.

At that time abuse of magic was even termed a parasite of the religions and was damned by the majority of the priesthood. It consisted in trying to force the gods to do something by the use magic powers, with the consequence that the gods then turned against humankind and accepted that the demise of their religions was accelerated by such misuse of magic. For this evil or black magic penetrated into the temples in order to break the enchantment of the gods, which in turn led to the destruction of writings, images and statues.

However, the wisdom of the gods is eternal because the soul conserves this knowledge and the soul never dies. Above all the holy trinity survived: Osiris, Isis and Horus. Many legends and myths clustered around these three divinities; they were often variously recited and told, often passed on in modified form, such that we would prefer here to limit ourselves to the essentials.

According to the papyrus rolls discovered, it can be assumed that the Egyptians themselves were hardly able to orientate themselves at some point in their mythical world. Their gods were so multifarious that they could no longer be classified into any stable system; many characteristics and deeds of the gods even overlapped, though that can also be said of the mythical world of the Greeks and Romans. So it may be helpful to briefly reconstruct the origin of the Osiris-Isis-Horus legend, since initially, even if it is more in a symbolic way, the sun god Ra was perceived as ruler as well as the creator god Atum. Both gods are one and nevertheless separate: Ra and Atum can be connected with the term Horakhty to Atum-Ra-Horakhty. The latter created Shu as god of the air and Tefnut for dampness or wetness. Shu and Tefnut in turn created Nut, the heavens, and Geb, the earth. Three of these gods we encounter in the final card, number twenty-one, of our Arcana. Nut is said to have with Geb created the more palpable gods, so that we can infer that the heavens and the earth bore the blessing and the salvation. Thus Nut and Geb were also seen as being the ones who had sired and born Osiris and Isis, that is created them; similarly Seth and Nephthys, who fulfilled important functions in the Osiris-Isis-Horus legend, though they do not seem so important for our initial knowledge.

OSIRIS

Osiris was perceived - after the creator gods - as the highest god of Egyptian legend; gods that are no longer concerned with the creation of the world but with life on earth. Very little is known about the life of Osiris; however, what is significant is the fact that the legends of the so-called "Götter zum Anfassen" (gods you can touch) show a process which seems to be transferable to humans, one which makes the gods to a certain extent human.

Plutarch, who, like Herodotus, was greatly occupied with the Egyptian religion, culture and developmental tradition, only tells the Osiris legends in bits and pieces, doubtless because they were not really familiar to him at that time. In the legend Osiris was linked to both sun and moon. His life was equated with the sun, his death and life thereafter with the moon; the dualism earlier mentioned also being reflected in this legend.

When Osiris (similar to Zeus/Jupiter later) achieved power, he introduced many reforms, but in doing so provoked the resistance of his brother Seth (cf. contrast between Zeus and Hades). Seth was the god of the desert and of heat - which need not only be seen negatively, even if the sun can also bring much destruction through heat and drought. Seth was always connected with the dog star, too, which was perceived as being responsible for heat. Nevertheless, this god was certainly viewed as one that accompanied the sun, even being protector of the sun, since he accompanies it up to its zenith/highest point. Thus many pharaohs, such as Sethos I, were named after him.

Due to the link to the dog star mentioned before, Seth was mostly depicted with a dog's head. This is reflected in the tarot set in card number XV "Demon (devil)". But it wasn't only his head which was dog-like, his body was sometimes also similar in appearance to an emaciated, but sometimes to a well-nourished dog's or jackal's body.

The positive aspect of Seth was that he announced the Nile inundations by means of the dog star, floods that made the land annually fertile and were therefore awaited with longing. When the dog star appeared at the beginning of August for the first time, just before the sun appeared in the sky, the Nile floods were announced. Now Seth did not want his position accompanying the creator (sun) to be disputed by Osiris. With 72 men (the number of precession, since the constellations - not the zodiac - shift by one degree in 72 years) Seth tricked Osiris and cut him into pieces. This is already the beginning of the relationship of the dead Osiris to the moon which is displayed in the heavens piece by piece, if we place the moon phases alongside each other.

Osiris was apparently defeated, no longer present, since his dead and dismembered body parts were scattered to the four winds. Seth, however, had not reckoned with the love of Isis for Osiris. She, together with her sister, Nephthys, searched for and collected up the scattered pieces. Nephthys, also seen in many legends as Seth's wife, could not approve of his murderous deeds (the sun burns the earth dry and cuts up the moon, as her light makes the moon visible in other parts) and so she came to Isis's assistance. Nephthys is incidentally also the mother of the Anubis-dog (son of Seth), which is associated with the judgement of the dead and the underworld.

With the assistance of her sister, Isis was able to help Osiris return from the dead so that she could receive and bear a son from him. Since Osiris was dismembered into fourteen pieces (the phase from the dark moon to the full moon in terms of the number of nights), it therefore also required fourteen nights before the reconstruction work was completed. Osiris now roamed between the underworld and the upper world (dark and full moon), was seen as lord of the night, but always returned from the darkness in order to prepare his son Horus, whom Isis had meanwhile given birth to, for the battle against Seth. This also explains why Osiris became God of the morning as well as of the evening sun, since the moon is consumed by the rising sun as the dying crescent in the morning, but is recreated as the resurrected crescent moon out of the setting sun. Whoever controls the setting and the rising of the sun, however, is Lord over life and death and therefore the highest of the gods that guide our soul.

Osiris thus demonstrated to the Egyptians in a most vivid manner that life does not end with death, but that the dead can all be resurrected. Osiris was the first resurrected god and was followed in many religions (in almost all of them in fact) by further gods, who taught resurrection. Yet whoever transforms from sun god to god of death and from god of death to sun god is both the role model and the measure of all things at the same time. This view became part of the soul's knowledge, revealed later as a wise saying in Egypt with the words:

> "As truly as Osiris lived, you live too. As truly as he did not die, you will not die, as truly as he will not be destroyed, you too will not be destroyed."

From this we can assume that almost all pharaohs believed that each individual one of them could become Osiris; and to become Osiris was the esoteric goal of every striving Egyptian, as numerous tomb texts and death rituals prove. This is also reflected in the Egyptian Tarot, in the cards of the Major Arcana, since card I also represents the beginning of the Way of Osiris. Osiris is always shown in pictures with a crook (a hooked shepherd's staff) and a flail (scourge) as attributes of rule.

These attributes symbolize the power of keeping a 'flock' together including by punishment. The symbol of the flail, the scourge, is clear; the symbol of the crooked staff is not quite so obvious, since not everybody is familiar with the fact that it developed out of the shepherd's staff. With a shepherd's staff is was possible to hook the foot or leg of animals that had run away or broken away from the flock and guide them back to the flock.

Osiris was on the whole perceived as a beneficent power. Even if people trembled before him in his function as judge, they always hoped for his mercy, which was equated with heavenly justice. For, although Osiris was resurrected from the dead, he never returned to Earth again. There he was represented by his son, Horus, who with his falcon was loyal to the gods of heaven, particularly to Osiris.

Osiris, who incorporated the connection between sun and moon within himself, depicted with his two horns as the image of the crescent moon, was for that reason also equated with the ram. Or rather the ram was viewed as the animal of Osiris and 'holy' functions were assigned to it. That is why many ram sphinxes decorated the ways to the entrances of the temples. Nowadays this can be seen particularly in Luxor and Karnak - a sign that the soul is renewed in the temple.

In Egypt two further symbols played an important part. The first is the cross with the handle at the top (*crux ansata*).

This cross is called the ankh cross and, stands as a symbol for life (ankh), which is why it can be found on each card of our tarot pack.

The second symbol is the Djed which is among the most frequent amulets of the dead.

This Djed-Pillar mostly shows a column or shaft with a four-part shape at the upper part of the shaft, but it can also be depicted with the human arms of the falcon god Horus or also with a sun disk or a snake. The Djed-Pillar is always perceived as the backbone of Osiris. It means: constancy - conservation - durability.

That much to the picture of Osiris who could hardly be imagined without Isis, at least as far as his resurrection and the conception of his son Horus is concerned. And so let us now turn to this goddess.

ISIS

Isis is the most important goddess of Egypt. There are indeed many others that we have already mentioned at various points, such as Bastet, Sekhmet, Nut and Hathor; however, Isis played the central role, comparable only with that of Maria in Christianity. Isis is certainly the predecessor of Aphrodite and Venus, but herself also originated out of the Babylonian Astarte. Isis incorporates everything which is projected into a woman that one worships. She was seen as divine lover, selfless mother, protector of all children; and she was even the god that was able to breathe life into people by using the draught of air from her divine wings - in short: she represented the universal divinity, of whom it was said:

> "... she was superior to millions of gods ... there was nothing that she would not have been aware of in heaven or on earth ... She was the mother of all nature, queen of all the elements, beginning and origin of the centuries ... the highest spouse, queen of the dead, the first occupant of heaven ..."

Isis was mostly depicted with the disk of the sun and with two bull's horns on her head. Her cult spread far beyond the borders of Egypt. Even in the later city of Rome, in spite of the related cult of Venus, there was an Isis cult. Isis had a sister, Nephthys, who we have already referred to, but who was never able to get anywhere near to Isis in terms of vibrancy.

Isis was above all protector of lovers and a votive goddess. The Isis priestesses played an important role in Egypt and held positions of power. No Egyptian woman would ever dream of getting on the wrong side of an Isis priestess.

Isis was - as were Seth, Osiris and Nephthys - born through the union of Nut (heaven) and Geb (earth). She was able to transform herself into a falcon, with whose wings she breathed life into Osiris, who had been reassembled out of fourteen dismembered parts. From this latter union emerged the falcon god, Horus.

The name Isis means "throne". That is why Isis is also almost always depicted seated on a throne. Frequently (though not always) she bears a child in her arms and mostly she holds the cross of life (ankh cross) in her hand.

Isis was also considered to be a great magician, for she possessed a rich knowledge and experience of magic wisdom, with which positive invocations were possible.

Isis was even able to change the destiny of people. Today we would say: she alone was able to take a severe karmatic fate away from a person in order to grant them a breath of good luck. Only she was in a position to override pre-determined fateful dicta or at least to modify and alleviate them.

ḋORUS

Horus was called Horakhty at first. Horakhty is the name of Horus, the child, which expresses the fact that Horus, the child fathered by Osiris and born by Isis, is intended to be a symbol of divinely interacting forces. Horus was always accompanied by a falcon which could fly to the sun (Osiris); however, there are also depictions which show Horus with a crocodile's tail symbolic of his connection to the waters of the Earth, more precisely of the Nile, which according to the opinion of ancient Egyptians originated from the heavenly Nile (the Milky Way). Horus, the god with the falcon's head, in which the eyes were particularly striking, was perceived as being both a god of the heavens as well as a king-god. His penetrating eyes symbolize sun and moon and alluded to his father Osiris.

Horus was pursued from childhood onwards. Seth hunted him with his seventy-two member band of followers so that Isis felt herself forced to hide Horus secretly in the Nile swamps (in the Nile delta). This is where Horus prepared himself for the revenge fight against Seth, a vengeful and cruel battle. Seth was said to have torn out one of the eyes of Horus, while Horus in response castrated Seth and was finally victorious.

Horus got his eye back again later, but the torn-out eye reminds us of the constellation in the sky at the dark moon, when the moon is no longer visible from the Earth due to being at its nearest point to the sun, which modern astrologers also term the 'burned moon'. Horus was always highly valued, especially as intermediary between Heaven and Earth or between gods and men. The intermediaries on earth were in this case the ruling pharaohs rather than the priests. It is also said about Horus:

> "... Horus the great god, Lord of the Heavens, son of Ra, who uplifts the sky, from which he was created."

Horus was also seen as the earthly incarnation of a godhead, yet not of Osiris, as it has sometimes been assumed. He had four heavenly children, who marked the four points of the compass and he was greatly loved by Ma'at, the goddess of justice and of the scales for weighing values, considered to be the daughter of Ra. Ma'at often wore an ostrich feather on her head. That was her symbol, since the heart had to be weighed in her name against that of a feather at the judgement of the dead. The heart was not supposed to be burdened with greater guilt than the weight of a feather.

VIEWING THE CARDS

Please note that how you look at the cards requires some training. This takes place less through any intellectual learning than by meditative observation and absorption of the cards into your soul. Quickly glancing over them does not achieve anything much even if spontaneous feelings and insights are important and need recording.

Combining the cards also needs practice. It is an advantage if you start by placing two (randomly selected) cards side by side in order to combine two pictorial statements and their content. It is appropriate to begin with the card which appeals to you least and then to place the card alongside it which you react most positively to. As a third step you might also place another card in between the two selected cards in order to see what could link the two chosen cards with each other.

Such exercises guide you best towards your own individual combinations, which in turn lead to important psychological insights. The card user will quickly feel to what extent the unconscious is involved in working with the pictures. The conscious mind now has to assimilate the unconscious impressions and convert them into comprehensible messages. It is important then to view the cards very intensively in order to absorb even small details and those seemingly unimportant aspects. Nothing is unimportant in the card image; everything has its sense, one which is often only realized after studying it longer. It is only via the so-called tiny details, which lead to an understanding of the whole, that it becomes possible to take the path in the direction of initiation; only in this way is it possible to expand the esoteric horizon.

It is worth noting the following procedure:

Firstly: *What does the first impression tell me?*

Secondly: *What impact does the card make on me spontaneously?*

Thirdly: *What does the card want to tell me?*

Fourthly: *Where does the insight the card provides me with lead me to?*

Four questions are put, each of which needs to be answered individually and separately. Only after doing this will the inner sense of the pictorial motifs become evident.

The next important thing is what the staff or wand, which can be seen on every card, has to say; also the transformation of the staff from one card to the other, since that is the way we can recognize most clearly the path of maturing with on the way to initiation. Here the name of the staff points out the destination most quickly. Furthermore the line of vision of the person depicted on a card is of significance. Thus we have to ask: where is the Magician looking, where is the woman on the lion looking, what is to be seen in the background? Of course the name and number of each card plays a part.

Everything we see, recognize or realize, everything that releases associations in us, is of importance. Yet we must also realize that our soul, our sub-conscious, assimilates something from the cards which is not yet at all clear to us consciously but which mostly leaves a very enduring impression behind it.

Everything in the pictures has a sense, is basically full of symbolic meaning; and sometimes it is good to look at the motifs individually, like the tessera of a mosaic, even though the whole picture should not be neglected. The individual cards represent a code which makes it possible to unlock one door after another on the way to initiation. Once all the codes have been broken, that is every door opened, we have meanwhile gained an insight into previously little known depths of the soul and its development - in general and individually. Each card reveals a secret which remains closed to the others (uninitiated) as long as they do not study these pictures.

What holds true for all the cards is that we should first of all delve deep into the motifs and that we should follow a particular procedure when looking at them.

Every card bears the symbol of the crux ansata, or cross with a handle, the ankh symbol. The word ankh stood more or less for life in ancient Egypt. The meaning of this term, however, went far beyond what we understand by the word 'life' today. Now we simply distinguish between death and life or vice versa. The ancient Egyptians, as has been previously mentioned, were convinced of the fact that life is immortal, which is why they also unconditionally believed in reincarnation. Their belief was certainly based on a solid inner knowledge, all the more since knowledge in their era was not only of a scientific nature.

The ankh symbol also contains the symbol of the sandal strap, a sign that we are continuously on the way. This sign consists of the upper loop with the cross strap and the lower strap. It certainly took a long time before the picture of the sandal straps had developed into the hieroglyph of life, but here it demonstrates the deeply symbolic thinking that once existed in Egypt and with which we must familiarize ourselves and get accustomed to again.

Since knowledge of eternal life was always taken as a matter of course for the ancient Egyptians, each of the tarot cards we have created with a feeling for this bears this sign – from the beginning to the new beginning. This also includes the so-called 'Death card', number XIII which here bears the name 'The Threshold'; for earthly death was always just a crossover or transition, a threshold.

Image, name and number of the cards also play a particular role, as does the staff which can be seen on every card - even if transformed into a wand, mace or something.

This staff symbolizes most clearly which stage of knowledge or development the searchers are at, especially when they are able to identify with one particular card. The staff also symbolizes which transformation of insight is being strived for, if for example one card is selected to represent a goal.

The staff is transformed more than all the other pictorial motifs; it even transforms away from being a staff. In many pictures it can hardly be recognized at first, as for instance in image XXI. The staff can then appear in abstract form on the images, especially in the second half of the Major Arcana.

The last 'staff' appears in a clearly recognizable form on card XI. In picture XII it is partly visible and partly hidden. However, from picture VI the staff sometimes appears in another independent symbol. Thus it is that our soul is transformed. It moves ahead only to relapse again before betaking itself upon the great Way. We recognize the staff - once more completely in the form of a staff - after picture V in picture IX once more and once again in picture XI, since we have here reached the middle card.

In this manner we are more capable of realizing, with the example of the staff and its transformed images, much of what opens up the meaning of the other pictorial motifs in the individual cards. Thus it is also quite good, when interpreting the Major Arcana, if a start is made with the staff image. However, it must be emphasized that everyone must find and follow their own personal way in such matters. These are only helpful hints.

In the following review the names of the cards are listed with the meaning of the staff relating to that card being placed opposite. Before the cards are interpreted, you should first read their names like a story.

	NAME OF THE CARD	MEANING OF STAFF
O - XXII	The Initiate	The Staff of Search
I	The Magician	The Magic Wand
II	The High Priestess	The Wand of Beyond
III	The Pharaoh Queen	The Staff of Protection
IV	The Pharaoh King	The Wand of Rule / Scepter
V	The High Priest	Thoth's Wand
VI	The Two Ways	The Arrow - The Ways
VII	The Chariot	The Reins
VIII	The Scales of Conscience	The Scales - The Sword
IX	The Hermit	The Wand of Light
X	Sphinx	The Obelisk
XI	Strength	The Staff of Leadership
XII	The Hanging One	The Scaffold with Sword and Staff
XIII	The Threshold	The Threshold
XIV	The Two Urns	The Ray of Eternity
XV	Demon	The Torch
XVI	The Tower	The Lightning Flash
XVII	The Magic Star	The Heavenly Nile
XVIII	The Moon	The Way
XIX	The Sun	The Tree
XX	Resurrection	The Instrument of Heaven
XXI	The Universe	The Goddess Nut

O-XXII. ᴛʜᴇ INITIATE

Number:

O - XXII

Transformation of the staff:

THE STAFF OF THE SEARCH

Motto:

IN THE BEGINNING IS THE END - IN THE END THE BEGINNING

0–XXII. ᛒHE INIᛒIAᛒE

The card which is called "The Initiate" is the only one to have two numbers, that is numbers 0 and XXII.

Both numbers are positioned outside the classical numbering of the Major Arcana, which ranges from I to XXI. (The numbers up to 21 were seen as particularly sacred, doubtless also because 21 results from multiplying 3 by 7) The number before, the zero, alone does not express anything in itself, although it symbolizes the cosmos and infinity. The number after, the XXII, indicates that the way is complete, but also that there is a new way in front of us. This number XXII becomes 0 again, even though it is at a higher level.

"The Initiate" card does not actually belong to the Major Arcana. Nevertheless, one can hardly imagine the tarot pack with out it. It is always the starting point. One can imagine the ways towards initiation (and beyond that) as a spiral staircase that we climb up – around one's own backbone, that of our body, our mind and our soul. Every way we take through the Major Arcana leads us a step or a level higher until we finally reach the peak. The goal is the inner pyramid. Pyramids were also places of burial – for the Egyptians knew that with every entry into the dark night a further new way opened leading to higher insight, to inner wealth of knowledge.

This was also known before the Egyptians, for building the Tower of Babylon symbolized nothing less than having to climb up step by step to get closer to heaven so that one will be taken up into the cosmos and be near to the creator.

All of this was no comfort for an early death, but inner knowledge that sought the sense in life not only in the one earthly life. That is what it is all about on this card. "The Initiate" may indeed have fulfilled certain initiation ceremonies, but he still has to strive forwards and make further efforts. Each time there are dangers lurking; each time the strenuous way is threatened by inner and outer uncertainties. This card then symbolizes the entry as also the exit, whereby the entry first of all has to take place within ourselves. The ancient Egyptians knew what was later, in the Middle Ages, a wise saying passed on to the young for their journey through life, namely that our luck lies alone within each of us – with a tragic aspect perhaps, that the starting chances are not always equal.

And yet – they are equal! Except for the fact that the one may have climbed several levels of the tower already, while the other has to repeat many a way once more. This is based on the deep fundamental insight of the Egyptians, which says that there is no equality for the conscious life on earth, and that this cannot be the case anyway, for a person has already taken many a way several times, while another is taking it for the first time; and yet another is already far ahead.

The souls of human beings wander eternally like the stars in their courses and encounter other souls, just like the heavenly bodies encounter each other thanks to their aspects. Those are the rhythms of the planets living in each of us, that is how the heavens mirror the spiritual in the individual as in the general. That is the secret which first has to be accepted however, even if we do not precisely know the solution.

A first glance at the card sees a man with his eyes blindfolded, walking blindly towards an abyss alongside a river (doubtless the Nile). He is holding his staff of search up high in his hand, since with it he would not be able to make ground contact below any longer. It even seems as if the man with the eyes blindfolded would be using the staff to maintain his external (as well as internal) balance. The step is hazardous and the crocodiles shown here as monsters are waiting calmly for their prey. The man is accompanied by a dog which has seized his tunic and wants to restrain him. In the background we see in addition an obelisk lying prone without any hieroglyphs, that is bare without any 'sacred' pictures. Above in stylized form an eclipse of the sun is depicted since the moon is darkening the sun.

The man himself seems to be young, is not poorly dressed, is carrying a (symbolic) bag as well as wearing rather impressive head-wear with the hint of an uraeus.

So much to the first, realistic 'glance'. But what does this image reveal to us beyond this information?

A young man has set out on an inner path. In order to find this path he has to concentrate on his soul: he must not be subject to any diversion, must not observe the superficial life around and let himself be distracted or led astray. As a consequence he submits himself to blindness; he relies on his inner voice, full of confidence that it (or a star which is, however, not visible) leads him. Only his instinct is alert, clearly embodied by the dog. The dog is not only man's most faithful companion, but it also symbolizes the animal instinct in us, and this instinct, which thinks of naked survival, is trying to warn the blind seeker. The pattern of the tunic which the man is wearing permits us to recognise that he knows his goal exactly. One pyramid after the other, one triangle above the other show that this man wants to achieve high goals.

The man at the start, however, also has a past, just as we also all carry a past inside us, a past which points towards the future. The future is shown here through the prone but as yet unfinished obelisk. The man is following the direction but at the risk of plunging into the abyss. We all certainly have to fall into our own abyss before we are willing to start out. Whoever realizes this can bear his head high despite dangers which lurk everywhere.

The initiate already knows the rules of play for this process. When there is an eclipse, independent of whether it is an eclipse of the sun or the moon, a god dies. This god has representatives on earth, either a pharaoh queen or king. These have to die vicariously when their god is eclipsed visible for everyone to see. At this moment the pharaoh's symbol of regency also falls, the obelisk.

The obelisk points both to the future and to the abyss, but the Initiate strides courageously forwards – even if still seeking, since his eyes are blindfolded. He relies on his instinct; and, indeed, whoever concentrates deeply on the picture, will discover that the dog only is apparently restraining the man. In truth the dog is leading him, guiding and steering him by small pulling movements on the tunic.

This means that we first have to rely on our animal instincts and must also accept them. The dog is an Anubis dog. We will be meeting him again at "The Scales of Conscience". Anubis was a son of Osiris, whom the latter had unintentionally and unlawfully procreated with the sister of Isis, Nephthys.

Isis searched for the child, and dogs which were leading Isis helped her to find the child. This child was given the name Anubis and was now supposed to guard the gods, as dogs did for humans. The waking instinct is then a gift of the gods which men should listen to.

This inheritance lives on in the Initiate who has delivered himself up to the divine in the broadest sense or has placed himself in the god's trust. Later Anubis guarded all the dead, who

25

stepped before the court of the dead, embalmed as mummies, and thus stepped into the presence of Osiris himself in order to be weighed both by Horus, the lawful son of the highest god, and also by Anubis, the son of Nephthys.

If the weighing came to a positive result then the dead person could continue on his way, even if he had to first of all pass through darkness. This darkness is symbolized here by the blindfold, which forces everyone to look inward in order to recognise himself. Anubis was also termed the god from the black mountain, which meant nothing less than that everyone who sets out on the way has to move away from the black mountain towards the light one.

One of the Initiate's hands is stretched forward, as if he wishes to say with this gesture: "I come with best intentions, accept me, whoever you may be", for none of us who sets out on the way knows who will encounter him and what will confront him.

In the picture we also see that the Initiate leaves the secure even if also precipitous ground beneath his feet; he is going directly into the water. However, out of the water all life emerged, according to ancient opinion. Water also represents the realm of the soul, as interpreters of dreams knew from those times and from the present. That is where our Initiate is striding to, indeed with dignified gait. He is no fool merely walking there for himself, as many later tarot cards show. No, this young man is consciously taking a way, however unknown it may be to him personally.

The one crocodile feels that this man is not his prey and turns away; the other seems to be ready to seize him, but his posture could also be a type of showing him respect. The ancient Egyptians did not only ascribe human behavior and gestures to animals but even raised the latter sometimes above human beings. Thus there was a crocodile god called Sobek. We have to live permanently close to the crocodile god, that means with the fear that the animal may make us feel. The crocodile was also equated with the sun, for in an old Egyptian legend it was stated: "because, just as the sun rose once out of ancient darkness... you (meant as the crocodile) have risen out of the primordial mud." So gods present themselves in awe-inspiring form, but whoever has no fear of them, because he trusts them, is accepted and even protected. Whoever feels himself to be blind but has nevertheless started on the way, need not suffer fear.

This is the conclusion of this card, which stands at the end and the beginning. A consoling card.

It encapsulates the factors:

> *courage and risk;*
> *blindness and yearning for sight, insight;*
> *trusting naiveté and relying on one's instincts;*
> *the new way which emerges from the old, even if the new way has not yet been found;*
> *longing for the other shore;*
> *the risk-taking of youth which, however, can still exist in older people;*
> *setting out from the depths;*
> *trust in the course of fate.*

The Initiate is on the way. Let us now turn to the first station of this way, the task not yet being known to the Initiate in his starting situation, indeed a task which is not yet allowed to be known.

1. THE
MAGICIAN

Number:

I

Transformation of the staff:

THE MAGIC WAND

Motto:

THE WAY IS THE GOAL

1. The Magician

The first glance sees a man standing at a table. In his hand the man is holding the magic wand which is also symbol for one of the four elements, namely for wood (earth). The sword as a symbol for the element fire is leaning against the table, while a dish that can hold the element water is standing on the table. In the dish we can see pieces of gold, which are a means of payment, as the symbol for the element air.* The latter may seem somewhat strange but the invention of money was one of the decisive achievements of the human mind – with all its negative consequences – because, through it, bartering was overcome, living together for people became easier and the economy could grow beyond the infant phases of naive primitiveness.

These four elements: fire, wood (earth), air and water played a decisive role in ancient times. They were also seen as being connected to the 'mind-human' since the fire element stood for the warmth of the heart and for the life-material blood. Wood stood for realism and the mastery of material things, the element air for everything mental and intellectual, while water symbolized the soul. Whoever sets out on the way needs to get involved with the distinction between these four basic materials.

The man in the picture called "The Magician" is looking to the top right, where he can realize the presence of the star which he is to follow.

His eyes are large and wide-open, the blindfold having been removed. The five-pointed star is still shining towards the goal over which a divine bird is hovering and which is delivering a heavenly message. The Magician is no longer accompanied by Anubis, the "dog of death", but by an ibis. The ibis in ancient Egypt always symbolized the divinity Thoth (as did the baboon), which means at this point that the time has come to set out on the way. The ibis (which does not appear quite real here since it has no legs) is accompanying the Magician, in a way floating by, as he passes a flower. Flowers were always seen as divine signs or symbols, as a decoration of nature which the gods grant us. Thus flowers will accompany us on the way towards initiation.

The Magician's tunic has the form of the seeking triangle, indicating forward direction, and he seems to be concentrating on the magic receptacle. The Magician himself is wearing a broad belt as a sign of concentration on the essential. This belt is held together by a snake shaped in the form of the lemniscate. The lemniscate was always a sign of immortality (as was the number 8, the Arabic form of which reminds us of the lemniscate). The lemniscate makes dualism and polarity evident: as above so below, left as right, the two halves which complement each other, such as light and dark, death and life.

The right hand of the Magician is directed upwards as if praying to the sky. One feels his gratitude for being able see again. This is the place to mention the fact that the way towards becoming an adept was always depicted with a young man. Of course the seeker can also be imagined as a young woman, but it always tended to be the men who were considered as having the vocation to dare to take the way towards the priesthood. The Major Arcana, however, clearly shows that women at that time were not suppressed but played an equal part in society.

In order to take in what the picture still has to reveal to us, it is a good idea to place the Initiate's card beside it. For here begins the way of the Initiate, who has made his first step.

Let us note that it is the same direction in which both figures look, from left to right; we can recognise that the way is no longer precipitous, but runs straight ahead, and we can feel the power of transformation which has already taken hold, once a person is prepared uncompromisingly to follow a new way. The Magician also has what he needs: Wand, Sword, Dish and Gold pieces, whereby the spiritual gold is meant here. It was never exclusively the case for initiated alchemists to transform physical lead into gold, but it was their opinion that every material, just as every soul, every mental connection contains a grain of the sun's gold, and that all dead material, soulless things can be wakened to inner, mental and esoteric life.

The right hand of the Magician reveals that the link to the past still survives within him, the gesture of his hands and arms expresses the fact that he still has his focus equally on past, present and future. Whereas the lights in the image of card O/XXII had grown dim, here the star which can be seen is shining bright. The heavens then show that they are prepared to observe the Magician walking the Way in order to give him the opportunity to develop towards initiation.

Here we are dealing with the card of Osiris, although Osiris is not shown. However he is always to be found wherever the seeker sets out on the Way. On the Magician's wand we see the stylized depiction of some flying creature which certainly is meant to make the magic connection between the divine bird (falcon) and the temporal bird (ibis) evident; Thus here too: as above so below, just as in the symbol of the dish both right and left find clear expression.

This, the first and therefore decisive step, is risked without the young magician knowing all the things that await him on the Way. Still he feels that he is more like a player, a joker, perhaps already believing that he is going to reach his goal quickly, although only one bloom has as yet blossomed in him (of 22 in total). Here we are still involved with a magician's apprentice rather than with a master; yet experience tells us that too many apprentices in life already consider themselves to be masters.

This card encapsulates the following factors:

> *the first step;*
> *focusing on the goal;*
> *the start of an action, a way;*
> *self-confidence being raised.*

The chance is offered to be able to go ahead, even if with the warning to be and to remain patient and cautious.

The Magician is still standing at his apprentice's table, which he will now have to leave behind him, since what is lying on the table must become his inner 'knowledge capital' since the gifts which are being offered have to be accepted and processed inside.

However, one more way begins with this card: **The Way of Osiris**

This Way – together with the Way of Isis and that of Horus – will be interpreted in summary after the descriptions of the cards; so that here it is only necessary to grasp what is symbolized by this picture: The divinity has breathed power and intellect into the seeker, has then created the pre-conditions, so that this Magician (whether male or female) now makes the effort to find her/his way to the divine.

The first step has been made, the step into the light, after which a step follows, which is intended to sharpen the Initiate's awareness of the dark.

O-XXII.   THE
               INITIATE

1.   THE
               MAGICIAN

---

*Mertz chose a different symbolism from the familiar interpretation of the Magician's requisites. The wand of wood is usually interpreted as fire (sticks were ignited, for example); the sword cutting and dissecting symbolized air; the gold pieces or discs representing all aspects of material stands for earth; the dish as a container of water represents emotions, relationships, the soul. Whichever interpretation you choose has no impact on the interpretation of the cards of the Major Arcana here.

11. тhe
ыidh pкiestess ☥

Number:

II

Transformation of the staff:

THE WAND OF BEYOND

Motto:

WE GO WHERE WE CAME FROM

11. The High Priestess

At first glance we see a priestess with an awe-inspiring black staff in her hand, sitting on a throne at the rear of the innermost temple – that is in the holiest of holies. Her look is veiled, nevertheless testing. The way to this priestess leads through a long gallery of huge statues of the gods – who reflect the contrast of light and dark. At the feet of the High Priestess (for she alone may sit in the holiest of holies) we catch sight of two flowers. The Initiate has thus reached the second stage. This stage is so formidable (as are the following ones) that the seeker does not appear in person at all; he is so insignificant and small as if he were not even present. The High Priestess does not only hold the long black staff, but also a papyrus bearing just a few hieroglyphs. She is sitting in all her bright glory on a dark throne, emphasizing how the black-white contrast pre-dominates here – despite the gold.

The frame within which the High Priestess has taken her seat emphasizes the light and the dark as well, even if in a rather abstract form, as is well expressed by the box-frame. It is night. The firmament shines bright, and on the High Priestess's head we can see the sickle of the moon as a head decoration bearing the dark sun (now set) through the night. We can also see the sickle of the moon on the staff, the 'wand of beyond', indicating that it is the soul that has stored the darkness within us, the apparently dead or passed away. The length of the staff reveals how long the way back is, how deeply we must listen into ourselves in order to assimilate and act out the inheritance living within us.

We can read on the sheet of papyrus (if we have been able to penetrate into the holy images), what we have suppressed in ourselves because it did not fit with our conscience, because we did not wish to burden ourselves. However, each person can only move ahead with light enough baggage. Or to formulate it differently: Whoever bears a lot of unprocessed burdens, will be so oppressed by them that moving ahead will be impossible.

This card wishes to warn us to search our soul, to accept our guilt and blame, and finally to do penance for it as well. The veil under the priestly head-dress shows that we must unveil ourselves before we can look the High Priestess directly in the eye. This veil has entered esoteric history as the veil of the Maja and demands of us that we have to research the secrets of being and of the beyond.

In order to see what the image may still reveal to us, we should lay the card of the Initiate alongside it. With both cards, at first glance, we become aware of the covered eyes. However, the eyes of the Initiate are intentionally and externally covered, whereas in this second step it is a question of illuminating the dark with open eyes in order to recognize it. The darkness, however, that lies behind us, is the same as what lies ahead – namely the Beyond.

Thus we have to review the darkness within us, where it has come from, the inherited aspects. The soul lives and never dies. It has stored everything. What counts now is to recognize what has been stored in order to build on its foundation; otherwise we have to start from the beginning once more. This is important to grasp quickly – at the start of the Way– since, otherwise, every way started presents a false way which only leads us into the labyrinth, not out of it.

The two flowers indicate that we must be receptive; yet we have already received without having learned anything much from it. Of course it depends here a great deal on the level and on the stage of development at which each person finds themselves. However, each person will realize for himself, if he searches deep inside what suppressed elements he must draw up from the depths and become conscious of.

The High Priestess is the priestess of Isis and she will take away a little of our fear of the darkness inside us. We can also name this card – in the modern sense – as the card of our karma, since we, as Sören Kierkegaard once formulated so accurately and appropriately: "have entered into the world with sealed orders". That means, a task is living within us, one we must discover for ourselves, though not in an external search, but while investigating our own soul. The priestess of Isis bears two star-shaped stylized blossoms on her clothing, which is also an indication about blossoming in the dark as in the light. The staff, the wand of beyond, is also held diagonally, it links above and below, as it does right and left.

The figure as a whole expresses the same, since the bare feet rest firmly on the floor of the temple, while the head stretches up to the sky, in which the heads of the divinities on the left and right are still more clearly outlined.

Karma says: What you have started you must finish. The basic start was to have developed out of the depths in the first place. Yet how shall we walk this Way if we shut ourselves off from our own many thousand years past?

Here we are dealing with the card of Isis, of whom people said: "there was nothing that she did not know, in heaven as on earth..." This sentence from the introduction should be called to mind here once again. Since Isis, as guardian of the soul, lives in each of us, we actually know everything – from an individual viewpoint – that we ought to know.

The second step then leads us back, makes it clear that there can be no step forwards without also having gone back. It was not without reason that the scarab became a symbol of luck and of survival among the ancient Egyptians for that very reason. Nowadays the section of the horoscope we call cancer points to the scarab beetle, since the same zodiacal section among the Egyptians was called "the beetle". Cancer, the crab, also symbolizes that there can be no real way forward without steps leading back. Thus it was that the crab and the beetle were selected as name patrons for that astrological section of the horoscope in which the sun has reached its highest point and must now move backwards.

This card encapsulates the following factors:

> *encounter with the shadow in oneself;*
> *researching one's own conscience;*
> *taking trouble over what the soul has gathered and conserved, its storage;*
> *transformation out of the depths;*
> *encounter with the soul as pre-condition for every insight.*

It is only now that the Initiate's thoughts can be clearly directed; with this card, depicting the second step of the Initiate's Way, the third Way also begins: **The Way of Isis**

The way will also be summarized after the description of the 22 cards in its various stations. However, it should now have become clear that this Way concentrates in itself the way of the soul. Thus the soul should be guided inwards, if it – and this is the decisive point – accepts this guidance at all. If it does that, then the second step is made for the Initiate, who can now dare to take the third step, a step which leads him rather into the real regions of this earthly world, since he knows that he has mind (Osiris) and soul (Isis) within him.

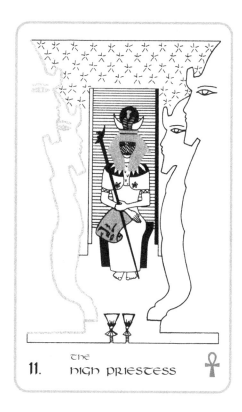

III. THE
PHARAOH QUEEN

Number:

III

Transformation of the staff:

THE STAFF OF PROTECTION

Motto:

PLEASURE IN LIVING GIVES ZEST FOR LIFE

III. The Pharaoh Queen

A first glance at the card shows a young woman sitting on a throne with a child on her lap. She, the child and the throne are all guarded by a lion. In her hand the woman is holding the staff of protection with the symbol of the crescent moon and the stylized sun at the top end. The young woman has an uraeus snake on her head as a decoration. Uraeus used to be a pre-historic goddess of protection from Lower Egypt. She was a goddess full of martial courage, used for example to protect the celestial eye of the god Ra, which referred to the light of the sun. That is why this ancient goddess used to wear on her head a symbol image of the striking cobra, which threatens, with its head raised to strike, to destroy anyone that attacks whatever she considers worthy of defence. We will frequently encounter this symbol of the uraeus snake. Here the first appearance indicates that the Pharaoh Queen has something to protect: namely the child, life's renewal. Procreated by the sun (Osiris), conceived by the moon (Isis), it is born here for the real world, and the new-born child needs the protection of the Queen.

She looks from left to right, straight into the eyes of the Horus falcon, for the child symbolizes the Horus boy himself. The sun is shining over everything – framed by the twelve stars, each of which stands for one section of the annual course of the sun. At the bottom right there are three flowers growing, each stretching directly upwards, focused towards the sun. The child is radiant, since it feels well cared-for, even if it still has its back turned towards the future, on the right, which is to be found in the direction of the Horus falcon.

The Staff of Protection wakens a distant memory of a 'scepter of rule', indicating to us that we are dealing with a ruler here, that is with a Pharaoh Queen. The Pharaoh Queens saw themselves as representatives of Isis on earth, also holding the child in a position familiar to us from the Isis statues. The connection of the Pharaoh Queen to sun and moon can be clearly seen from the moon, just as from the Horus falcon, perching on an elevated stone shelf, the link between light and darkness towards the earth is also symbolized. The Pharaoh Queen is wearing a head-dress that expresses the same thing. This is a card expressing courage and vitality, while the tame lion guarding her also shows that we can meet life with courage and joy when we have tamed our animal nature, however majestic this latter may sometimes seem.

The beginning for doing so is self-restraint, not to take oneself so seriously, but to focus everything on what is to come, on the newly born. This factor we may approach in turn as feminine, inner reasoning.

If we place the card of the Initiate alongside, we discover that the line of sight once again fits – i.e. the view into the future. The High Priestess lets the Initiate pass by while observing him; the Pharaoh Queen helps him to find the Way. For at the third stage, too, the seeker is still like a child that has to be helped, for whom those that rule have to be examples.

What does this picture still reveal to us at a deeper level? First of all, the eyes of the woman are wide open once more, as with the Magician, and a knowing smile, such as only mothers have, plays around her lips. Whether gods smile (visibly) is something we do not know, but whoever has been cared for by a god has reason to smile. Being able to laugh has always been seen as a gift, but also as a distinction for human beings, being an expression of what clearly and visibly distinguishes humans but also gods from animals.

The Egyptians always saw their kings as humans, just as the kings felt themselves to be children of the gods but humans as well. Thus tyrants could hardly be imagined as long as belief in the gods filled the soul and thereby animated all action. It is true that the kings had to demonstrate supernatural abilities during their lives, but they knew how to do this in such a way that the human aspect never fell by the wayside. In that sense the rulers of Ancient Egypt can still be role models for us today.

The connection between the rulers and the priesthood functioned relatively unproblematically (apart from exceptions during the era of Achenaton), since the senior priest was mostly the first among the ministers, being what we would term a prime minister today. Ambitions for power from one side or other were then the beginning of the end; they also started a turning away from belief itself and from the initiation into esotericism connected with that.

The Pharaoh Queen's robes are regal, even festive, as if she has dressed so finely especially for the initiation of her Isis child. The child knows, without having realized it mentally, of his importance, something all children have inside them if they are not hindered in their zest for living, which is a natural gift, by hardness and strictness. The Pharaoh Queen has the task of guarding their vitality, their zest for life, and thus of guarding the possibility of living itself. This involves feminine intuition, dedication to justice, which does not yet have anything to do with the law and the conventions for living together. Here is the fourth stage, then; but the Initiate has only taken his third step at this point.

This third step is then the step into real life, the step into the probationary period; for the powers of survival will be schooled and trained, since with upbringing and education from external sources, a person's self-education begins.

With this card we encounter the demands of our earth, without neglecting our view of the heavens when doing so. Whoever places "The Initiate" alongside this card can see that the Initiate has set off on the right way, even if he needs to see himself here as a mere child on the road to initiation.

This card encapsulates the following factors:

fulfillment of duties and obligations;
nurturing and guiding love;
conservation of life,
integration into a social community;
it is all about the female reality, which is not comparable to that of the male.

This third step on the Way of Initiation is simultaneously the first stage of the fourth Way: **The Way of Horus.**

The child of Osiris and Isis leads us increasingly towards life's realities. These stages will also be examined in context later. The word "reality" is only correct to a limited degree, nowadays being the symbol for an all too material attitude. Esotericism, too, every belief, indeed even love itself represent a reality which reaches clearest expression in the concept of love. Love cannot be described, neither measured, nor grasped, but it is still there. It links people more strongly with each other than any other reality can. Love is unconquerable as long as it is firmly anchored in the hearts of two people. A reality, from which perhaps those realities can some time emerge, to which Horus wishes to lead us. Horus is perceived as the earthly incarnation of God. In order that people may have a comprehensible idea of the power and the will of the divine, he encounters people in the form of a falcon, so that they are led on the right path. And, as we can recognize in the next picture, the falcon has visibly taken over the guidance.

IV. THE PHARAOH KING

Number:
IV

Transformation of the staff:
THE SCEPTER OF RULE

Motto:
WHOEVER CONTROLS HIMSELF CONTROLS HIS WORLD

IV. The Pharaoh King

A first look reveals a Pharaoh who is indicatively looking to the right. The Horus falcon that was still looking opposite to the line of sight in the previous picture, Card III, is now sitting protectively at the back of the Pharaoh's head and is focusing on the heavenly bird, which brings the light of the sun with it. The Scepter of Rule is being raised towards the future – i.e. to the right. The right hand is open, reserved, emphasizing some instruction or other. Pharaoh is sitting on a block of stone, on which four flowers are depicted, two of each leaning both to the right and to the left. Just like the Pharaoh Queen, the King is wearing a uraeus cobra on his head, one which does not seem to be just petrified and reactive. The throne in the form of a square-sided stone shows some hieroglyphs, that means sacred pictures, while in the middle we can see the symbol of striving, the divine triangle.

Card III, The Pharaoh Queen, still plays a significant role here. However, one difference becomes evident: the Pharaoh King is not taking care of one child or of this one in particular; he rules in a wider context. His scepter is longer than that of the Pharaoh Queen; at its tip we can see the princely symbol of trinity and the sun symbol that every pharaoh has to embody and possess if he wishes to rule his realm. His eyes are wide open and directed to the front; there is a marked concentration, reflected in his facial expression, while he looks ahead. This pharaoh seems very composed overall, indeed dignified; he is aware of his leadership role.

The bird plunging down out of the heavens, as if guided by the rays of the sun, is focusing on the pharaoh with his falcon. One ancient image of the heavens was that depicting the wings of a falcon stretching over the world. Sun and moon were perceived as its eyes. The sun was also conceived as having wings and was even drawn that way in ancient times, that means the winged sun, such as we can still see it above the temple doors (especially in the Middle Kingdom) or as the crowning finish on memorial stones. Thus dead falcons were also mummified, since they were considered to be the incarnation of the god Horus, a view which led to mummified falcons being used as escorts for the dead. No wonder the Ba of a person, that means their soul, was often depicted by a bird with a human head, symbolizing how the soul starts after the death of the body on his way in order to fly to the astral spheres in heaven from which it searches out a new body that it brings to life with the first breath.

The size depicted for the sun bird indicates how closely pharaoh and sun bird are linked to one another. The falcon with its sharp and warlike beak is a predator which seizes its prey, its characteristics later being used by humans to advantage "with the blessing of the sun", as it says in one ancient document. No bird in ancient Egypt caused so much fuss as the falcon, if we ignore the ibis for a moment; though even the latter never became quite as important. The ibis also came from the heavens, it is true, but as the bird of the heavenly Nile – the Milky Way – not as ambassador and enunciator of the creative sun, without which no life would be possible.

What does this picture also reveal to us in a deeper sense? It is also about the transformation of the triangle into the square, that is about conjunction, or as it was later described, as the heavenly wedding of mind and material, since there was always the firm conviction that material without mind would be lifeless, mind without material would only create a dream world. This profound esoteric wisdom lies hidden in the throne of the Pharaoh King.

If we now place the Initiate's card next to this picture, we know what experiences have to be mastered here for learning and initiation. After absorbing female reasoning we now have to learn and comprehend male reasoning, one which has to extend beyond the immediate progeny. That is also a reason why the Pharaoh King follows the Pharaoh Queen. And just as the dam defends its own offspring unconditionally up to the point of sacrificing herself, the leader of the herd or pack always has to keep an eye on the overall well-being of all animals. Consequently we are freeing ourselves a bit from the excessively individual viewpoint, looking at the wider framework, the greater context, if we should claim to play a leading role.

The human being is naturally subject to challenge when doing so, for we have to realize that, if necessary, our own interest must be deferred, which may often require heavenly assistance. This card, then, also symbolizes the authority which is only genuine, if the person who exercises it, masters himself, defers to other factors. Whoever considers claiming the right of leadership, must be able to perform more or must have dedicated more work than all the others. Only having been born to be a leader has never been enough – not in that era and not today. In this sense the times have not changed so much.

The Initiate is still seeking blindly, while the Pharaoh King is looking with knowledge into the distance. Now – as we realize in advance – it is a question of personal decisions, for which we must, however, be mature. Furthermore, this card wishes to convey (just as Card III has already done) that earthly life must first be mastered before we can spread our (inner) wings in order to set off towards the sun. The Egyptians also knew their sun challengers, just as the Greek myth of Icarus later tells us. In card IV the heavens descend to the Pharaoh King, whose look is not directed at the heavens, but is straight ahead.

The fourth stage completed here is based on the following factors of interpretation:

> *authority;*
> *father figure (which can also be assumed by a woman);*
> *trust in the future;*
> *supportive activities;*
> *self control;*
> *belief in the power of the gods and its realization on Earth;*
> *fulfillment of duty as a basis for any entitlement or claims for rights;*
> *danger of presumption and arrogance.*

The Way of Osiris

This card still represents one stage of another way, that of Osiris. The god encounters us again at this point; he who has led the Magician and has now made him ruler – as we might infer in this case. On the basis of his magical capabilities leadership has now been allotted to him. Here it must be stated that the concept of the Magician has modified considerably over the millennia. Nowadays magician is almost a professional term for a conjuror or illusionist, who wishes to simulate a different impression of this world. In earlier times the magician or magus was always considered to be master and controller of the four basic elements, which is what is expressed in Card I. Only after mastering these is it possible to ascend to roles of authority, though it need not be the position of the pharaoh himself. Yet we are always concerned here with obtaining authority born of performance.

If the gods did not exist, the rulers would abuse their power, an ancient Egyptian once wrote (roughly translated) when recounting a legend. He announced such a deep truth to us that still holds true today, even if this is not always in the rulers' awareness most of the time. Card IV should be understood in this sense.

O-XXII.   ᴛʜᴇ INITIATE

IV.   ᴛʜᴇ PHARAOH KING

V.   THE
     HIGH PRIEST

Number:

V

Transformation of the staff:

THOTH'S WAND

Motto:

ALL AND EVERYTHING HAS ITS TIME

V. The high priest

A first look sees the High Priest raising his hand as if to test something or to swear an oath. He is holding his staff in the other hand. It is the only time that the staff is related to one specific person who can be named. This staff is of a dark color, but is also formed as a lengthened ankh sign, which tells us that life always goes on, whatever happens with time.

Next to the throne, which has the form of a chair and is no longer shaped as a simple square, there are two people sitting, a woman and a man. You can see that one person has dark clothing, one light; here it is completely irrelevant whether it is the man or woman who has the light-colored clothing; it could just as well be reversed.

It is a question here of two fundamental distinctions which refer to magic. In Card IV we came to the conclusion that magic powers belong to leadership. In this card, however, the hazardous aspects of magic are pointed out, namely white magic and so-called black magic. In Ancient Egypt black magic was also rather familiar, and it increased during the period of general cultural decline to such an extent that the priesthood was no longer able to ban this type of magic, which was an abuse of magic power.

The High Priest knows about this danger and that is why he is warning the dark-clothed person with his raised hand while holding his staff of life (ankh) against the back of the light-clothed one. Both pupils - and they are only pupils kneeling in front of the master - have already learned a lot, so that the female figure knows about the male, as the dagger in the clothing indicates, and he in turn is aware of the feminine, shown by his wearing an ornament.

The High Priest provides his services as a priest of Thoth, indicated by the ibis which adorns his head. The ibis was always the announcer of the fruitful season. It announced, as did the scarab, the arriving Nile muds and thus saved the lives of many a simple fellah.

The god Thoth is god of the fourth dimension, time. Thoth later developed into Chronos and Saturn. Whoever rules time, rules all: also the sciences, experiences and karmic processes. There is only one thing time cannot do: create life. For that reason alone, the god Thoth is not the highest deity.

Above we can see a sun shining, for, by marking the passage of the sun, time became measurable for humans. The symbols of rule, the obelisks, also served that purpose. For their shadows functioned like the hands of a sun dial, which, by the way, very much disturbed many a ruler as they still had to live with a time of uncertainty in that era. If there was an eclipse, they had to die. It was only through the astronomical calculations of eclipses by the priests of Thoth that eclipses could also be predicted. This then led to the possibility of the pharaoh's looking for a sacrificial substitute, mostly their first born.

The card reveals more to us through its background, if we place the picture of the Initiate alongside it. Just as he had to pass in front of the High Priestess the Initiate here has to pass in front of the High Priest, who observes him critically. The High Priest does not indicate the right direction with his look, as the King and Queen Pharaohs do, because here it is the question of an inner development, that of the soul.

There are five flowers blooming already at the feet of the High Priest. They extend in all directions like a chalice. His legs are clearly discernible, the knees being especially prominent, something emphasized still further by the two kneeling figures. The High Priest requires prayer. Prayer is done in a humble kneeling posture, since one does not meet one's god upright; that is in a posture ready for fighting. When kneeling there is no need to lose one's dignity. But to bend one's knee is an indication of respect, which is indeed due only to the gods and should not be demanded of any others. Whoever kneels will be blessed. That is how the Priest's gesture with his hand should be understood.

The High Priest is reticent. His mouth is half closed, since not everything has to be stated explicitly. The size of his slim figure reveals to us that we are dealing here with an over-sized figure whose connection with the heavens is made via the headdress, which means that no other connection – such as via a bird – is required here.

All of this forces us to consider our own insignificance, compels us to an inner humility in the face of the huge obelisks, of which one seems to rise from the depths, the other stretches far up into the heavens. The obelisks stand upright. The Initiate, who is walking past a lying obelisk has then progressed quite some distance so far. It is the fifth step being completed here, the stage of testing. At the next stages the Initiate will not meet any more priests or pharaohs. From now on he is left to himself at first. This High Priest, of whom we cannot be sure whether it is merely a priest or Thoth himself, also reminds us of this fact.

The following aspects are taken as a basis for interpretation with this Card:

> *the laws of time;*
> *the testing;*
> *the temptation of black magic to save time and exercise power sooner;*
> *overcoming of inner fears;*
> *self-check of one's own maturity.*

This Card which also symbolizes the five senses (Card number five) represents not only the fifth step on the Initiate's Way but also the second step on the Way of Isis.

Isis, who embodies the feminine, thus the receptive soul and who can also – like Osiris – release us from the realm of darkness, had her own priesthood, which was similarly organized to that of the god Thoth. Isis in particular required the development of the soul, the maturing of the powers living within us and which were already present before birth. These powers, however, which can achieve more than all the real possibilities of a human being, have to be very specially trained; and the pupils must be subjected to particularly tough testing for this reason. The soul does not recognize any laws of time, since it does not die but the immortal within us must not – as we shall be seeing – be surrendered to the demons.

That is why the second stage of the Way of Isis is particularly important, for whoever does not get control of his soul must go back a long way in his development and has to learn again and again, until the guardian of the threshold, divine Thoth, makes the way free for him to move up.

In this way Card V builds on II. Noticeably similar is not only the name of the card but also that both are equipped with the ankh symbol. Thoth was originally a moon god, and the moon also helped people to measure time and to recognize their souls. Both are being tested here, for the next step leads to the first individual, i.e. personal decision for the seeker searching for maturity. If the test is passed (Card V), we can expect to achieve this maturity.

O-XXII.   THE
            INITIATE

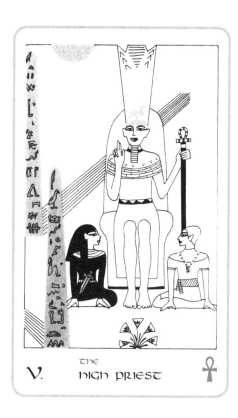

V.   THE
       HIGH PRIEST

VI. THE TWO WAYS

Number:

VI

Transformation of the staff:

HEAVEN'S ARROW

Motto:

DOUBTS ARE FRUITFUL — ETERNAL DOUBTS DESTRUCTIVE

VI. The Two Ways

The first glance sees the erstwhile Initiate with his view directed to the front. The man beneath a starry sky has arrived at a parting of the ways; he is faced with the choice of taking either the way into the darkness or into the light. The two women bear witness to the fact that each way has its shadow sides or its light ones. The women are not trying to win this man's love, so they are not nude but rather modestly dressed. The man is also not looking at either of the women. You can see that here it is more a question of the two souls (that are always feminine) which are causing the man some confusion in choosing his way.

He is tied at the feet by the lemniscate, which indicates that both ways must be taken for walking towards eternity. At this point it is only the question of which way to take first, for it is obviously impossible to walk both ways at the same time.

The dark way is rather one returning to experiences made in the past, the light way leads into the future, but both belong together. The lemniscate around the man's feet indicate this convincingly. On each side of a way there are three flowers in bloom: the divine three, the symbol of the pyramid, is shown along both roads then.

Out of the heavens there is an arrow pointing down towards the man's head. Heaven's arrow is not directed towards any particular connection, not towards a woman, not towards the (or a particular) heart – but exclusively towards the head. The heavens expect a decision from the rational mind.

The erstwhile Initiate has been led to a point where he has to make his own decisions on his own responsibility. It is required of him personally, now after he has been trained and tested. The 'two souls in his breast' (as Goethe termed it) each attract him in their own direction, and – to emphasize the point again – both souls are aware of the right way. It is more a question about which step in which direction should be taken at this point. That's where the dilemma lies. The path of search has reached a fork; there is no signpost to be seen; the man has to find the right indications within himself. (One can just as well imagine this card with a woman in the middle, but in ancient Egypt it was primarily the men who were first called upon to become adepts. From the viewpoint of meaningful content it focuses on the person confronted with a decision).

Decisions are difficult to make when doubts gnaw at you. Decisions are necessary because they warn you of being too self-confident, something which we are going to meet for instance with the next card. However, every doubt must be worked through and then cast aside by making a decision, doubts inwardly conquered.

The sense of the card becomes still more evident when we place the Initiate alongside it in his original manifestation (card 0). At that point he was 'blind', even if it was on a voluntary basis; now his look is pointing straight into the future. (The future always lies to the right of the observer for us.) The Initiate remembers the past here, remembers what is now, such that he can make decisions for the future. This card also represents the last possibility of deviating from the path that he has now set out on. The man can still turn back because he has not yet encountered the true secrets which lead to initiation. The deeper sense of this card is found in this view.

Formulated in a more modern way we might say: the trial period has been successfully completed and is now finished. If the future adept wishes to seek further on the chosen Way, there will be no return. Whoever cannot stick to this Way can no longer go back to the original circle of Initiates, but will have to serve the circle of the Initiated without really belonging to them.

Ancient Egyptian history is full of examples of this development, since those who did not achieve initiation mostly had to fulfill their service in the temple, shut off from the outside world. No wonder doubts arise for anyone who has reached this point. For, alongside the promise of belonging to the Initiates, there is the risk of having to serve as a slave. Indeed this means no chance of ever being able to rise up into the higher regions, however perfectly and belief-driven the service has been mastered to the satisfaction of everybody after that point.

That is what it is about at the sixth step. It is the jump over to the other side of the river, without the possibility of turning back, though it is not an earthly death which is meant here, even if this can already be seen as a pre-test for the true step across the Threshold to be made at a later point. And just as the lemniscate symbolizes polarity, we here have the two ways which can be followed, each way seeming attractive and of value. The man is standing consequently before a self-assessment, which can mostly be solved, in the esoteric sense, by meditation with questions directed to the self. For the decision must be made, as the arrow indicates, with a clear head, that means not while being intoxicated or in any condition approximating intoxication. The 'not yet initiated' here (this is how far the Initiate has reached) is not even permitted to put his question to the stars, which is why he has turned his back to them.

To state it clearly once again: the man can still turn back. If he goes ahead, towards the right side – then the return route must be trodden too, but then through a process of inner mastery. Often involving a denial of temptations, for the Initiated must deny themselves many earthly joys, without regret and without complaint.

Thus the following interpretation factors emerge here:

> *the life decision, as well as decisions in general;*
> *doubts and the consequences arising;*
> *the training of the rational mind/reason;*
> *intellect;*
> *the ability to deliberate and assess;*
> *the question – the answer;*
> *the freely made decision;*
> *the leap to the other shore.*

This sixth step is at the same time the second stage of the Way of Horus. Out of Pharaoh Queen's child (card III) a young man has emerged, who has completed his introductory training and is now in the process of deciding his life's calling. All the great Pharaohs (but even the lesser ones) perceived themselves to be Horus, thus son of Osiris and Isis.

Card VI is also to be seen as the connection to the divine, which can indeed really mean that the Initiate, in striving to move onwards, has to fight for the deity or at least has to make sacrificial offerings to it. For every man (and also every woman), who wanted to make any career in ancient Egypt (as we might express it today) the question arose as to whom they wished to serve in the religious and mental sense. So, if a Pharaoh turned to a certain name based on that of a god, he evidenced publicly his origins, which pharaohs gladly derived from a particular god with a good conscience – such as Pharaoh Sethos, for example, whose name is derived from the god Seth. The headdress of many pharaohs also indicated an inner connection to a deity.

So, now from the little Harpokrates – standing for Horus, the child – the adult Horus has emerged.

O-XXII.   THE INITIATE

VI.   THE TWO WAYS

VIII.   THE CHARIOT OF
         OSIRIS

Number:

VII

Transformation of the staff:

THE REINS

Motto:

WHOEVER DOES NOT REIN HIMSELF IN CANNOT STEER

VII. THE CHARIOT OF OSIRIS

A first look sees the Initiate standing on the chariot of Osiris, which is moving at full speed. The Initiate has now made his decision; he wants to move ahead, wants to be initiated. That is why he is seized by such restless emotions that he has climbed onto the Chariot of Osiris (symbolically), which is under the protection of the stars. Now the Initiate is already holding the signs of rule in his hands, the crooked staff (the shepherd's crook) and the flagellum (the scourge). Neither of these can be used by him as he rides the chariot impatiently.

That is why he probably has to apply these instruments of power on himself at first. The chariot is travelling at full speed, as the raised shaft and chariot axle indicate, although the chariot bears a heavy load. The charioteer (we can perhaps imagine the fabled charioteer from Delphi here) is drawing a light and a dark sphinx along with him. He is still accompanied by the light and the dark, which he will never be able to get rid of, for if we look closer we realize that the dark sphinx is basically the shadow of the light sphinx; for, if there were no shadow, there would be no light either; if there were no light, shadow would never be visible. The dark is our shadow then, mysterious as the sphinxes that – whether visible or not – accompany the Initiate on his way towards initiation. The charioteer steers his vehicle very impatiently, since he is running down seven flowers which remain behind damaged. That means the self-discipline which is necessary in order to steer the Chariot of Osiris has not yet been achieved.

We can penetrate the meaning of the card still deeper by placing the image of the Initiate alongside. The Initiate directs his gaze upwards but risks going towards the chasm, his Way leading downwards. The charioteer is also directing his look upwards, though no longer blindfolded; but for him there is only one goal, and that lies in the heights. The whole picture reveals his upward striving. His self-assurance has grown after he, the man, has learned to make decisions. Decisions always lead one onwards, even if they are mistaken or not the most diplomatic. But life demands decisions, and the decision in favour of initiation is particularly challenging and fruitful. The worst thing in life is never to have come to any own decisions, because this leads to becoming incapable of acting on one's own responsibility.

Not being able to decide means letting yourself drift, allowing your fate to be taken out of your own hands. This is a particular characteristic of the masses, who swing from jubilation to grief, from temptation to depression. Our man has decided, and even if some flowers should be run down along the way, this decision moves him onwards. One thing to be noted is that the use of the reins is skilled and knowledgeable. This can only be achieved if a person has previously learned to rein himself in.

We can see the lemniscate, by the way, on the clasp of the belt and perhaps remember that this was shackling the feet of the doubter in the previous picture. Now the lemniscate focuses the centre of this man, as in the image of the Magician; now, however, the lemniscate has been earned, whereas previously it had only been a potential. And this lemniscate is placed horizontally, leading to the centre and being the centre at the same time, also repeating here the significance of light and shadow against the dark belt. How similar the charioteer has become to the Pharaoh and the High

Priest is shown by the beard decoration, which only indicates the closeness to these role models in a symbolic manner since the Way to either of these roles lies far ahead still. That's why the chariot is driving at such high speed.

However, the charioteer radiates confidence; he has overcome his fears; he seems to have been reborn. For we are not only reborn from one life to another, but we can experience rebirth several times within our own lives. And whatever is true in the microcosm is also true for the macrocosm, the supra-dimensional, for if what is below is to equate with what is above, then the reverse is true: as above so below. This man wants to move ahead! The Chariot of Osiris was always perceived as a chariot of victory. Only those on earth who have achieved the greatest victory over themselves may use this chariot.

To the person who has conquered himself comes an unbelievable power, of which those people, who have not taken up the struggle with themselves, have no idea and indeed should have no idea. In other words, all those people who have not learned to apologize for themselves, who are not able to correct themselves, who always think they are right, who believe that everything centres around themselves alone. They may steer as self-righteously as they wish – they will still not be spared the strokes of fate. These people are damned not to realize that every blow of fate comes from inside, never from the outside, that every person is himself responsible for his own fate.

Now the Initiate has really overcome the beasts (the crocodiles) and also knows that there is no return. Thus his back is free; sense completely directed to the fore, the ballast seems to have been cast aside. However, it is not enough just to have cast it aside; that's what the two sphinxes remind us of.

Self-confidence leads to self-confirmation and own impulse to act. If the latter is forgotten, the self-confirmation fragments, and we would then return to the zero point, the very start.

Therefore the conclusions for interpreting this card are easy to draw:

> *self-confirmation;*
> *courage for the future;*
> *self-conquest;*
> *readiness to act;*
> *danger of arrogance and pride;*
> *impatience in relation to achieving the goal;*
> *verve and readiness to confront the difficulties;*
> *conclusion of the learning process.*

We have arrived at the Initiate's seventh step, thus reaching a divine number that pairs up with the divine three; for the third stage of the Way of Osiris is here linked to the seven. Three times seven makes twenty-one, those being the learning steps of the Major Arcana.

From the Magician (first step on the Way of Osiris) and the encounter with the ruler Pharaoh (second step on that Way) we are now permitted to climb onto and steer the Chariot of Osiris. Osiris is the god of reforms, thus of transformations. However, every transformation or reform first begins with the individual himself. That is what it is all about at this stage.

We can now understand how the man on card VI has transformed into the one on card VII. If the self-transformation is not achieved, then we have to change ourselves without the blessing and the further guidance of Osiris, which is hardly attainable. There is no way in which this will be adequate for the Way of Initiation by which we hope to draw nearer to Osiris; for it is towards him that we are steering his chariot.

Osiris lives in all of us; we only have to discover him in ourselves. We can only manage this, however, when we have discovered and really got to know ourselves. Who truly knows himself – when everyone believes that they know themselves already? We need divine power to be released from this error and to be redeemed.

O-XXII. THE INITIATE

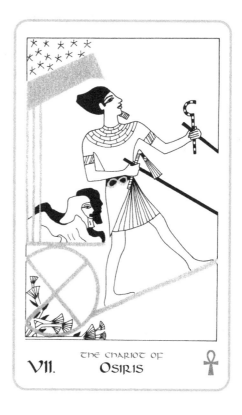

VII. THE CHARIOT OF OSIRIS

VIII.   ᴛʜᴇ ꜱᴄᴀʟᴇꜱ ᴏꜰ **CONSCIENCE** ☥

Number:

VIII

Transformation of the staff:

THE SCALES – THE SWORD

Motto:

ONLY THOSE WHO HAVE A HEART CAN WEIGH HEARTS

VIII. The Scales of Conscience

At first glance we can see the extra-large scales with the silhouette of a woman's head behind them. Nowadays we would speak of Justitia, but here in fact it is the head of the goddess Ma'at. Her eyes are covered, even though she is not wearing a blindfold, by a sword lying horizontally and the cross-bar of the scales instead. The Horus falcon that can be seen at the top right helps us to realize that the huge head is that of a goddess. The falcon is also watching over the conscience-weighing process – which is the focus of this stage. The mouth of the goddess is full-lipped, that is full of life, indicating that she knows quite a lot about earthly temptations.

At the foot of the scales there is a sheet of papyrus with some notes about the life of the person whose heart is being weighed. The heart is lying on one pan of the scales. The balancing weight is indeed light, for it is a feather: a stylized ostrich feather of the goddess Ma'at. Ma'at herself personifies all-embracing law, which includes truth, order, harmony as well as all the small elements of justness in the cosmos, indeed everything to do with the universal order. Whoever became a priest of Ma'at was simultaneously the highest priest in the land, wielding substantial power. Ma'at was considered to be a daughter of Ra and at the same time to be ultimate truth, a truth which extended far beyond what we humans think we can find in our civil law. This is what Ma'at rules about in Osiris' court of justice, for every god owns their own court of justice in order to be able to weigh justly there.

There are numerous depictions of the Judgement of the Dead coming from the most varied epochs and often depicted very differently. The heart is always weighed, but not in the sense of a bourgeois morality, not according to a law that people have constructed purely from their rational minds in order to find some order for living together. No, here it is more the question of the over-arching framework which the religions later took over. For here the sinners were sooner forgiven if they regretted and did penance, rather than the self-righteous, who claimed for themselves the right to interpret divine law according to their pre-conceptions. Here it is more a matter of justice in the sense of maturity and development. That is why this card is placed in position number VIII, i.e. rather early, such that the future initiated can be reminded that one day everything will be weighed, also the impatience which was expressed in the previous card, also pride and arrogance, which are not punishable according to earthly laws.

At the foot of the scales we can see the dog or jackal-like god, Anubis, that is often considered to be the weighing official. He is together with Ammut, the devourer with the jaws of hell, which is due to be fed the heart if it is found to be too heavy. In this particular case, however, the heart does not seem to be any heavier than the feather, so the seeker may be permitted to continue striving to attain his goal of initiation. Notable is the fact that the weighing of conscience is handled by animals, even if it is done under the supervision of Ma'at, the daughter of Ra. According to divine law humans should not treat animals as being of little worth and should not kill them frivolously and cruelly.

We understand heart in a symbolical sense as meaning the good, love, the heart that we can give to another or that is as hard as stone. In Egypt, the heart means the seat of consciousness and moral will – and this is what is weighed by the animals and their gods. If the heart passes this test, the eight blooms at the foot of the scales can continue blossoming and stretching upwards towards the sun.

We can penetrate still more deeply into the symbolism of this card if we place the Initiate's card alongside it. Noteworthy are the eyes which are covered in both cases by an external source. In this way we can sense that the Initiate has reached a decisive stopping point with his eighth stage. It is in fact the last station but one. Unburdened by the outer world he started his Way – while looking inwards – and now encounters Ma'at, the daughter of Ra, who also does not judge him from an external viewpoint. And the Initiate once more encounters the crocodile that has also been following him up to this point, maybe hoping that the Initiate would perhaps fall prey to him in the end.

This picture still has one more particularity of interest. We encounter two forms of staff here. The vertical weighing rod is a staff, the horizontal sword is the second one. With these two together we have the cross that points in all four directions and is the symbol for 'as below, so above', 'the left as the right' and all other pairing and polarities. However, the sword also expresses the fact that one must fight for justice. There is no justice without struggle. Up to this point the seeker has possibly been able to manage without fighting, but now he has to take up the struggle, which does not necessarily have to do with warlike conflicts. However similar this card may be to the Judgement of the Dead, in the Major Arcana it is not about dealing with a dead person, but about an indication of the truth that one day we all have to face this court. And each one of us has the personal opportunity to justify himself, though this is not even necessary in fact.

The direction of the gaze is also important here. The goddess Ma'at allows the seeker to walk past her; she can feel whether he is afraid of continuing ahead or not, or whether his stride has only hesitated for the moment.

The following indications for interpreting the meaning of this card are:

weighing of the heart;
weighing things up consciously;
searching the conscience, particularly one's own;
need for harmony;
critical inward examination;
the struggle for internal balance, equanimity and emotional harmony.

This eighth stage is also the step out of the external lemniscate into the internal one, since number eight – written as an Arabic figure – mirrors this complementary symbol.

This is well expressed in the symbols of the animals in this picture; for we see the creatures of death and hell below, but above the creature of the sun, of light: namely the Horus falcon. These creatures balance each other, as do feather and heart, as do the handle of the sword and its blade, the decorative head-dress of Ma'at. And the flowers weigh up what has been, lying behind us to the left, whereas what is to come can still be expected to our right.

The eighth step also represents the third stage of the Way of Isis, as the High Priestess (card II) and the High Priest (card V) have prepared the Initiate for the great test (card VIII). Isis also stands behind this goddess in card VIII, for Isis is to a very considerable degree concerned with the heart. Also emerging from these three stages is an indication that nobody has been called before this decisive court of judgement quite unprepared. Whoever came before it defended him-

57

self with negations, rather in the following manner: "Neither have I caused suffering to people, nor put injustice in the place of justice, never have I tipped the weighing rod in my favour, nor sinned against nature ..."

The defence went something like that and, if what was stated was true, the pans of the scales remained in balance. If it was a falsehood, the pan with the heart dipped downwards, to be noted by Thoth or his priest (card V) for further consideration.

However, our seeker evidently has permission to move onwards.

O-XXII.   THE INITIATE

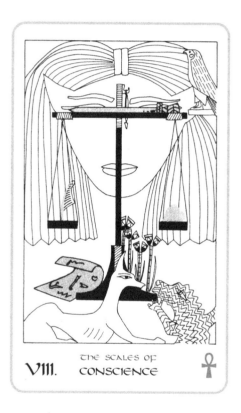

VIII.   THE SCALES OF CONSCIENCE

IX. THE HERMIT

Number:
IX

Transformation of the staff:
THE WAND OF LIGHT

Motto:
WHOEVER IS ALONE NEED NOT BE LONELY

IX. THE HERMIT

A first glance sees a tall man in a dark-colored garment. It is our Initiate, who has changed considerably since the encounter with the goddess, Ma'at, and whose way is nearing its end. We shall say goodbye to him, leave him with his light shining inwards, that is introspecting. The seeker is carrying a very long staff which reminds us of those of the High Priestess and the High Priest, but the upper part has now been worked with an ankh symbol with threefold wings which point both forwards and backwards. In his left hand he is holding his lamp. In ancient Egypt bringing light into the darkest corner, for example by guiding sunlight into a dark cave or excavation was a well-known procedure. A further mirror picked up this light in order to guide it around a corner. In this way the sun could transport the light of day into many a dark region via various reflections. That is what it is about in this picture, where everything seems to be dominated by a huge symbolic mirror.

At the bottom snakes appear and they seem to have been attracted by the light. By means of the light which he has ignited within himself the seeker is looking at the snake demons that live inside him and which he has not previously paid attention to. Three flowers with nine blossoms are growing out of the depths as a sign that even with but a little (inner) light the darkness inside a person can be brought to flower and thus to fruitfulness. For out of each blossom a fruit can emerge. The man's gaze is directed towards the right – that means towards the future.

Looking deeper into the symbolism of the card can be done by placing card O - XXII beside it. In both cases the man is alone with the beasts. But the creatures on card 0 are ones which appear in the external world, even if the dog also represents the person's instincts. The beasts on card IX, however, are symbols of demons that inhabit a person's inner world. They are snakes such as vipers and cobras; that means evil thoughts, temptations, envy and whatever else can eat away at a person from the inside. This will no longer harm the man, since he has turned his light onto these creatures consciously and thus illuminated them. They still try to make the seeker afraid, for the snakes are rearing up threateningly, though they cannot really reach him.

We can see in picture O - XXII that the Initiate has blindfolded himself in order to cast his gaze inwards. Now he is looking inwards but no longer needs to cover his eyes in order to do that; he can look outwards, forwards and at the same time inwards. Thus he has made a huge step in his development. The Initiate's Way is indeed completed, without his having reached initiation yet. But that is not the relevant matter at this point.

The seeker is alone, occupied with himself. Now there is also a danger, if one is only concerned with oneself, introspecting - something which must really be done from time to time, in order not to lose the connection to the basic animal instinct. The dog that we see on the Initiate's card (not the simple Anubis dogs within the series from I to XXI), has done its duty; with its instinct it has wakened that of the seeker, who then recognizes himself as such - also a creature of instinct - and learns to understand himself. In this regard everyone has to make his way alone, having to accept his solitude. This does not mean being lonely, however. For whoever has set out on the Way will always find people to accompany him: protectors, helpers; at most, he is out-wardly by himself, but never inwardly.

Every seer, every prophet, every person who wishes to see beyond what the everyday horizon reveals to him, has to – as ancient and biblical role models show – go out into the wilderness in order to be alone with himself. This is the rule which must be obeyed: living in seclusion with yourself. That is when the powers of regeneration are revealed, which can only be drawn out of one's own soul.

This is the courage that the seeker has to find. Mostly it is attempted nowadays via medita-tion, but basically meditation circles around thinking, around the positive thought, whereas with real seclusion, cloistered with oneself, it is a matter of recognizing the evil within oneself. Every thought about polarity and dualism leads to the realization that evil confronts good, indeed that one complements the other. Who can know what is good if he does not know evil; who can as-sess what is already evil or what is still good? Are the basic drives good or evil or, when are they good, when are they evil? Here there is much overlapping, for good is not always the task that has been listlessly and half-heartedly completed, although for instance it may have served the cause of procreation and conception. And something not serving reproduction can be thoroughly full of relish and excitement. This is only one example of many.

Is eating evil if more is eaten than the body needs or if taste increases the pleasure in eating? When is the yearning for delicious nourishment evil? Is it so when somebody is starving who is not permitted to eat as well?

When is the use of magic powers or of esoteric knowledge damaging? Is it only when that leads to the dark regions of black magic? This can never be clarified generally; there is no norm that applies to all; that is something which can only be experienced and realized by everyone for himself.

Consequently we can record the following points towards the interpretation of this card:

looking inwards or introspection;
insights;
recognition of one's own demons;
the Way through solitude;
asceticism.

How these clues and indications are realized is each person's own affair. That can be achieved via dreams; indeed the dream way is one of the useful modes of insight. The ancient Egyptians were well-known for the fact that dreams played a major role in their awareness; pharaohs always had interpreters of dreams at hand, not only to assess the future correctly, as the dream reported in the Bible of the seven fat and the seven lean cows demonstrates. Dreams are perceived as the language of the soul, but also as the language of God, one that is largely forgotten nowadays. The Egyptians knew about these languages and thus cared for them.

The Initiate has now reached the end. From the following card onwards the Way of the Magician begins, and he is now making his first step. However, the ninth step of the Initiate is also the third step on the Way of Horus, and this development seems logical: cared and protected as the child of the Pharaoh Queen (card III), developing toward the doubter (card VI), to become now the seeker into one's own self (card IX). According to this card, Harpokrates, the child Horus, has become a man. Old depictions show Harpokrates as an infant, holding his mouth closed with its finger. It is a gesture expressing that nothing should be permitted to emerge that is not yet mature. Here is also one more secret of initiation to be identified: not to speak too early about things that we have indeed seemingly understood but not yet really grasped. The Hermit has now reached this point of maturity, thus terminating the first Way of in total seven Ways.

XI.   STRENGTH

Number:

X

Transformation of the staff:

THE OBELISK

Motto:

THE WHEEL OF FATE NEVER STANDS STILL

X. SPHINX

At first glance we see a wheel that is divided into twelve parts and thus reminds us of how the zodiac is divided. The wheel turns – as does the zodiac – and two creatures seem to be chained to the wheel. A dog baring its teeth has to go downwards, a human – naked and hairless – wants to go upwards. This means: the dog-like must descend to the depths so that the human, also naked as he is, can be reborn from the depths. Naked stands for the concept that here everything burdensome is left behind, that evil remains in the underworld, full of snakes, so that the good spirit can rise up again with the human being. At the bottom there are also ten flowers blossoming, for with this tenth card we have almost arrived at the middle of our Way, indicating that now the decisive phase is beginning. This also becomes evident by the fact that, in comparing developments, card I, the Magician, must now be placed alongside the next ten cards. However we are not yet that far.

The wheel is tied up to an obelisk, which was the model for the shadow indicator of a sundial. The shadow also turns from morning to evening as if it were fixed to a wheel. The obelisk is covered with sacred pictures, hieroglyphs. We already find ourselves at a very advanced period of ancient Egyptian culture. Dominating everything we see a sphinx, which can be male or female. We know that the male sphinx was familiar to Egypt; while in Greece the sphinx was almost always female.

However, the gender is not really so important, not even if we are dealing with a lion, bull or horse sphinx, or even with a snake sphinx. What is of importance - for the sphinx always had a guarding function - is: what is a particular sphinx guarding? Always something sacred, something divine. The sphinx always watched over proclamations and revelations, about promotions or advancement and demotions or relegations. Pairs of sphinx were even often used if the task was to watch over trees of life or sun symbols, for example.

Our sphinx guards a rising and a falling process, viewed from the outside – but the relegation or descent phase has to lead to a cathartic cleansing, while the ascent or promotion phase has to show whether this has succeeded. That is what the male or female sphinx is watching over. Such a sphinx was always located in places that were considered particularly sacred; let us remember the Giza Sphinx in front of the Cheops and Chefren pyramids. A sphinx would also be found on the throne, but in particular next to images of the gods.

In our pictorial motif the sphinx seems to be very aware of all around and also does not look grim but rather friendly, as if it wishes to benevolently greet the person who is trying to ascend. The sphinx, also a provider of riddles and conundrums, watches over and steers the course of initiation; that is its function. It holds the snakes at bay and thus also symbolizes the polarity of the light and dark gods. For it stands for the sun-god while the snakes stand for the moon-gods. (The moon always had more gods than the sun, doubtless because the moon appears so changeable in its various forms.) It was only in Greece that the sphinx became a harbinger and even a witness of the event of death. That is why it later developed to guarding tombs. In the sphinx we can then recognise, in the higher sense, divine vigilance.

It also symbolizes the office of guardian of the gateway into the esoteric world of secret sciences, so that not every person can simply stroll in and out.

As this card is the first step on the Magician's Way, let us place the picture of the Magician alongside it. The Magician is handling the symbols of the four elements rather thoughtlessly, like a magician's apprentice might. Now he encounters the Sphinx, experiences something of the rise and fall of a development, a maturity process. The Magician, still doing his thing quite in the radiant atmosphere of the sun-bird, is now forced to see that people have to go down into the snake-pit in order to rise reborn out of this pit. And this is not just once, but constantly, in fact as long as the dog-like in them has not fully died away and been overcome; indeed until the seeker, the Magician, can no longer be controlled by dog-like drives. The Sphinx, seeming to look down from the heavens, also watches over these experiences.

The wheel of fate that turns for everybody also wishes to make clear that it all depends on one's own fortuna, which everyone has to find within himself. That means in the ancient Egyptian sense: everyone has to solve the riddle the Sphinx has given him, his own personal riddle. And not solving it means: down into the snake-pit, again and again, until you understand which Way now has to be taken. Up to now all the tests and trials were more of a mental nature, but here the whole person is challenged, here it might also require physical stresses and strains. For the demons once more grab at you, something those people in particular know who have been threatened by some addiction. The Egyptians also knew of the dangers of addiction, and it can also be an addiction to want to know everything too early. Whoever strives upwards can find himself at risk: that the striving to ascend becomes no more than an addiction to reach initiation at top speed, to belong to the selected elite as early as possible. However, still more dangerous is to know too much at the wrong moment. That is one of the greatest dangers that a person might encounter because he can hardly resist such a temptation.

So we can record the following interpretations for this card:

working on oneself;
effort and struggle;
stretched on the wheel;
the crisis;
the insight and burden of a temptation;
exertions.

This first step of the Magician means that magic forces are now in play, the seeker might now be able to play still more with the fire. The fire - and here inner fire is intended - must now be dominated and simultaneously kept alive.

We are at the fourth stage of the Way of Osiris since the first stage, that of the Magician, has been directly integrated here.

The Way leads onwards via the Pharaoh King to the Chariot, and now to the Sphinx. That means that the tests and trials required on the Way of Osiris are becoming ever more demanding. Up to now the way has only proceeded upwards but now comes a threat from the depths, for the riddle of the Sphinx prevents any rapid ascent to Osiris. And every Egyptian – whether initiated or not – wanted to become one with Osiris; that was the highest goal. The fact that this goal is not supposed to be easily attainable is ensured by the Sphinx's guardian function.

In that sense this card from the Major Arcana represents the greatest crisis on the way towards initiation. Even when someone has imagined that he has attained the goal – it has not been attained. No-one should fall for this deception of a quick career, a rapid ascent, a fast-track acquisition of knowledge and a sudden grasp of esotericism and magic. This is the crisis that everyone goes through, where you ask yourself whether everything up to now has not been in vain. Only after overcoming this crisis is it possible to make a new attempt to ascend further. In this sense seekers have a similar experience to mountaineers, who – having reached one peak – discover a still higher one that they feel compelled to conquer as well.

Now we have reached the middle of the Major Arcana.

XI.   STRENGTH

Number:

XI

Transformation of the staff:

THE STAFF OF LEADERSHIP

Motto:

STRENGTH COMES FROM THE INSIDE

XI. STRENGTH

With our first glance we can see a woman who is standing, almost like a dancer, on a powerful lion, which in turn is moving from right to left past eleven flowers. For the first time - exactly in the middle of the Major Arcana - the direction of gaze on a card is completely different. If the divine figures have looked straight at the observer till now, if the seeker, the person readying himself for initiation, has aligned himself from left to right, then here we encounter the opposite. What does that mean?

The card is called "Strength". After the experience that everything always has to be renewed, that nothing lasts forever, Strength, based on inner strengths, grows - enabled by this inner acceptance of the law of constant movement. Now that it encounters him, the seeker can rely on this strength. The woman on the lion is approaching the seeker. Her expression is peaceful, even friendly. There is encouragement in her look. The threateningly long staff that we know from the High Priest, the High Priestess and the Hermit has lost all its threat. It has transformed into the staff of leadership. Without touching the lion this staff nevertheless guides it, which expresses the fact that it is more a matter of mental leadership.

The lion was always called king of the desert; he was the symbol of the sun, since he was able to withstand the utmost heat of the sun and his mane reminded people of the sun's rays. This lion with human eyes is coming towards the seeker, wishes to make his strength available, a strength which also comes from the complementary polarity of the woman on his back and which should encourage the seeker to do further deeds.

It is not without reason that the sphinx was mostly depicted with the head of a lion, or at least with the body and paws of a lion. And the lion was seen as the power which was able to convert acts of creation into reality.

The Egyptians were also familiar with lion gods. In particular we should mention the goddess Sekhmet, who was called the angry eye of the god Ra. She was seen as a goddess who brought misfortune, who announced death, who called down evil luck and epidemics into the world if the divine will was not fulfilled. Indeed, she even threatened the destruction of the human race. Thus all Egyptians honoured lions and lionesses at all times as gods but were in awe of their strength and dangerous potential.

The headdress of the Pharaoh Queen reminds us of the lion's mane and shows that the sun's rays deserve honouring. Apart from that, in the old kingdom, the lion goddess was seen as the divine mother of the pharaoh.

Alongside Sekhmet (meaning powerful) the cat goddess, Bastet, was also worshipped and her appearance was quite leonine in feature as well. Bastet was linked to the cow goddess Hathor and symbolized the peaceful side of the lion goddess. She also became cat goddess because people tended to perceive peacefulness as a feline characteristic, even though cats are unpredictable, something which cannot be said about the larger members of the cat family such as lions.

Sekhmet and Bastet also appeared as sister goddesses; thus they symbolized on the one hand the dangerous, on the other the peaceful. The lion cult led to the mummification of cats, just like humans, after their deaths, which meant that great cat graveyards arose, which can still be visited today. Lions and lionesses were seen quite specifically as companions of the god Ra, and the legend goes "... that Ra sought out lions to use their strength against the enemies of the sun-god..."

The lion on card XI, led by the woman, comes towards the seeker from right to left.

Let us then place the Magician alongside, for he is taking the second stage here along his Way. He raises his Magician's staff or wand as a greeting in similar fashion, and we can note something of a formal but overall friendly motion.

The Magician, and thus the Initiate, who has opened his eyes for the first time, is filled with strength, meaning inner strength. Now the symbols of the four elements gain in power for the first time, too: the sword, the cup, the wand, gold discs.

The sun-bird soars in the same direction as the woman has taken on the lion; whereas the ibis, while approaching the lion, now intends to express that, with time, strength grows and increases. So both these cards, Magician and Strength, placed alongside each other express great confidence and a well-founded trust that the right Way is being taken. Fear has been overcome by inner security; there is a conviction that inner strength can operate peacefully, that the greatest strength that can be imagined - symbolized by the lion - can be tamed by gentle, female, and thus sensitive, skills. Here indeed some dressage has succeeded, something humans have always (unfortunately) striven for in vain; it is doubtless dressage that only the initiated can master, having been trained quite specifically to become a role-model for situations when the skill is required to ward off dangers with determination and to ensure peace. Struggles have to be shifted inwards, every battle first having to be a struggle with the self; then all other battles will be victorious and achieved without applying force. The seeker can now continue his way with inner confidence and deep trust.

This results in the following interpretation for card XI:

strength;
self confidence;
mastery of own drives;
exultation;
trust in God;
sureness;
being at the peak.

If we have a look at pictures I and XI alongside each other, the Magician is already experiencing the rise and fall that was prophesied by the Sphinx in picture X. However, he is warned not to believe that he has already made it. The steps of the Magician go more in leaps and bounds, as far as the inner development is concerned. With each step forwards higher demands are automatically made; each person must be ready to adjust to more complex situations, must train his intuition. Apart from that we are looking at the fourth stage of the Way of Isis here.

The fourth stage is the middle in each case (i.e. that applies for the Ways of Osiris and Horus as well). Card XI is the indisputable middle of the Major Arcana, so we can recognize the significance of its being the same as the middle of the Way of Isis.

We have been following Isis now on her way via the High Priestess (card II), the High Priest (card V) and the Scales of Conscience (card VIII) to card XI "Strength". This clearly underlines the fact that the subject concerned is the strength of the soul, of the inner - immortal - strength. Initiation is not only acquired for a life on earth but is pre-learning for the distant way via reincarnation to more distant realms. The earthly being has become of no importance; the soul is preparing itself for a world, in which silence speaks 'eloquently', so that 'I enter into thy realm of the spirit, which illuminates me forever.'

XII.   THE HANGING ONE

Number:

XII

Transformation of the staff:

THE SCAFFOLD WITH SWORD AND STAFF

Motto:

LIVING "BELOW AS ABOVE" WITHIN US

XII. THE HANGING ONE

The first glance reveals a man who has suspended himself of his own free will on a kind of wooden scaffold frame. He is alive and does not seem to be unhappy with his situation. We may realize from the attributes of sword and staff, from the tumbling coins as from the pan into which the coins are falling that we are confronted with the Magician here, that is the seeker who has betaken himself to this somewhat strange position. At a first glance we cannot see any flowers, but then realize that these flowers have transformed to gold pieces - or vice-versa.

The Magician is looking back, seeming to want now a moment of reflection on his Way; but by this he also indicates that he has understood the rise and fall involved in the Sphinx's task. Having perhaps just been at the top, now of his own free will he has adopted the position of looking at the world from below. In doing so the position of his legs indicates that he has undertaken this troublesome task consciously to support this inner effort, since his legs intentionally form a triangle. His hands are crossed over each other but there is no sign of any cramp. The ancient Egyptians knew how necessary vital and alert thinking is and realized that for this there is a pre-condition that blood must flow into the head to invigorate the brain, and thus to avoid (metaphorically) bloodless or abstract thinking. In order to be close to the heavens, one must assimilate the earth deep within oneself. Whoever wishes to go upwards has to know where he comes from, what it is like at the bottom, where his roots are.

The Hanging One shows from his position that he has understood what it means to be anchored mentally, and not just now - but forever. If this awareness represents the truth, it will hardly depend any more on an attitude, a physical position or position in the world, unless the position in the external world were to be of significance for Initiates, since it is their attention which must be gained. Indeed, whoever gets others to look up to them one day, must have learned at some time to have looked downwards or into the depths.

The law of reversal, of complementarity, becomes clear once again and this law ran through the whole of Egyptian literature. Thus it can be read in certain texts: "beggars have become lords over treasures; he who could not make his sandals, is now a man of property..." Or "...the rich grieve, the poor rejoice, gold and lapis lazuli are draped around the necks of the servant girls. The bodies of the noble women are insulted by the rags they have to wear."

As the reversal of everything was perceived as a certainty, it was quite natural to occupy oneself with this reversal quite early, to trust its significance and even to anticipate it. Being initiated means being informed, and he who is informed is always one step ahead.

The second half of the Major Arcana begins with this picture of being upside down, if we consider card XI to be the middle. The beginning of the second half of man's life is always linked to a crisis, however, something which the oldest experience of life reflects. For in the second half of life, its crises are revealed with all clarity. They have to show themselves, since otherwise development would not continue, for crisis (derived from its Greek origin) means nothing else but development. Thus a crisis should not be avoided, but should be accepted, even received as a gift.

"...I believe that everyone knows equally little of the gods..." was a remark once made in the histories of Herodotus. It was just for that reason that those striving were searching for the acknowledgement of the gods. However, one thing they could be certain of was that the godly lived within them, that they had to discover the divine within themselves, which is why - just like the stars in the sky - they moved through the dark. And just like the sun reverses its course when it has reached its most northerly or southerly point, thus humans also had to turn round again. Indeed not only humans. They experienced - and often with a shudder - that the fertile muds returned at the beginning of summer with the Nile floods, that the waters flooded over the banks, an event many creatures - whether human or animal - learned at the cost of their lives. But then the time came when the waters receded, filtering down into the soil, so that the land by the Nile became desert again, which once more emphasized the lack of fertility of the land in the winter and spring months. And the Nile - that was a conviction they were certain of - came from the heavens. Indeed the phenomenon we know today as the Milky Way was called by the Egyptians the heavenly Nile, from which the earthly Nile originated.

When the waters reversed, when drought now and later flooding ruled the land, this was a further indication of reversal, one which related to the day and the night, to life and death. Indeed the death card follows directly after our card number XII.

A deeper understanding of this card is made more accessible if we place alongside it the card of the Magician, who is taking his third step here, that of turning upside down. We can see the same requisites, though the Hanging One has here freed himself from everything unnecessary, even from the lemniscate. However, his hands are simulating that fact, by the right hand indicating left while the left points to the right, the wrists touching at the crossing point. Thus the arms and hands imitate the eternal symbol of life, that of the snake.

Over the scaffold the sun and moon can be seen facing each other as complementary opposites. The Hanging One has placed himself in this "sacrificial position", thus honouring both celestial bodies. The position is certainly one of sacrifice, as are many positions of prayer, but it is not a sacrifice made because a sin has been committed. The Hanging One does not then symbolize - as often stated in many modern tarots - any kind of punishment; on the contrary!

We may note the following interpretative elements:

turning upside down;
revolution;
new insight;
change;
the "as above, so below";
the transformation of the Magician.

The Magician's third step here is simultaneously the fourth stage of the Way of Horus.

The Way of Horus very clearly shows human striving. As a child he is protected, still being called Harpokrates (card III). As a man he suffers doubt and seeks to order his thoughts (card VI). As the Hermit he looks deeper into himself (card IX) in order to gain a new and complementary picture of the Above and Below by offering sacrifice (card XII). Here too at the middle - because the fourth - step of this way we are coming to the decisive transformation.

One more thing is important for understanding the reversal of position. The living never lived without the dead. Again and again contact was made with them, above all many appeals were directed to them. The living also knew that whoever does not look after the dead wastes his own reincarnation. Consequently everything was seen as part of a great cycle, as celestial bodies and nature revealed. "To realize the impact of the stars I do but need to study the fruitful or infertile soil." This ancient experience was a decisive indication for understanding the world process, and this ancient experience is being pursued by our Hanging One in order to grapple with death (the next card).

XIII. THE THRESHOLD

Number:

XIII

Transformation of the staff:

THE THRESHOLD

Motto:

DEATH IS LIFE — LIFE IS DEATH

XIII. THE THRESHOLD

A first look reveals the scorpion goddess Serket with her symbolic animal (water scorpion) on her head (nowadays we would be speaking of a heraldic supporter in the form of an animal). Her arms are spread wide. This gesture says that she is offering an invitation to enter her kingdom - beyond the threshold. There we can recognize sacred pictures (hieroglyphs), as well as two heads of dead people, who are looking with empty yet seeing eyes at their protector. Serket (also Greek Selkis) welcomes the dead, in fact as the protector of life. She opens the door of her threshold both for those wishing to enter and those desiring to leave. We read in the Egyptian Book of The Dead: "Hark - hark: the bolts of the mighty door are shifted - now I am permitted to cross the sacred threshold."

This Threshold also gave the card its name. Later card XIII of the Major Arcana was only identified with the term Death. However, the way in which we understand this term in general nowadays, namely as something final, was not the way the concept was once understood. Death represented in earlier times a longingly awaited crossover. It was indeed forbidden to take one's life - for everyone had to cross the threshold at his appointed time bearing his own experiences - but it would never occur to any ancient Egyptians to believe that death was an absolute end. Of course the Egyptians could also see that no new life could be expected from the mummies themselves, but they knew that the Ka survived, which is why air-ducts were constructed in the tombs and pyramids, so that the Ka could escape through them.

The mummies were, however, always respected (apart from by tomb robbers), for in ancient Egypt it was also said: "Yet never disturb the sleep of the world."

This emphasizes the belief that it was the privilege of the gods to wake the body to new life. For the progeny there was only the duty of embalming the dead so that they were equipped for immortality. It must be evident to modern man that the Egyptians did not overcome death, yet experienced it most profoundly as a necessary function in the universal whole: "only death can reverse the aging process to which all being is subject".

Here, too, we encounter the concept of reversal, one which is of such great import. As the night in the south is almost as long as the day or vice versa (depending on the position of the sun), the passage through the dark was depicted as the passage through the realm of 12 hours. For the night, the dark, was full of life. Thus the thirteen blossoms here reach out towards the realm of Serket, since they, as part of nature's living things, seem to be aware here that this darkness does not lead to their withering and decay. The indication about nature's creatures seems relevant at this point because every belief in another life in the hereafter arose out of observing nature, where everything in fact constantly returns.

The goddess Serket was also "...born in and of nature". Originally she was a goddess that appeared as a water scorpion and who was attributed the gift of healing poisonous bites of such as serpents and scorpions. Thus even at that early period she brought those already dead back to life and rebirth. So whoever can heal on earth, such that death is overcome, will be especially capable of doing this work in the afterlife. Thus death loses it fearfulness. The process of dying was seen as being one of pain, a suffering before the threshold, that may not be shortened, if the time which Thoth, the god of time, had allotted for each person, had not been completed.

Dying is a task which has to be completed with dignity. Both of the heads in the realm of the dead make this evident. Even should the sun go down, it will surely rise again; even should the moon darken and vanish, it will be reborn as a sickle moon and become a full moon once more.

The card says: whoever wishes to be initiated, has to believe in a beyond the threshold; he must not fear physical death, but the spirit must be directed far out into the more remote cosmic regions, since the souls become stars or the stars offer the souls a home, until they resolve to develop further by means of another body, another mind or spirit.

Thus it is not surprising that the dead rest much more peacefully than during their lifetimes or that in the extensive graveyards of Cairo the living actually live among the dead.

The realm of the dead was **the** reality for the Egyptians, the here-and-now on the other hand only a transient world of illusions. Here lies the secret which the people of our age find so difficult to access.

In our picture, seen from the viewpoint of the observer, the future lies to the right (as incidentally in all other card games). The past lies to the left. This represents ancient Egyptian wisdom, for "...if death is breathed into a person's left ear, he is bound to make the step through the gate of death..." where the soul was able to find itself again in its old and now once more fully functioning body. This basic idea of living and dying, of birth and death never basically changed, at most only certain elements of the death cult.

We can more completely understand the depth of this card if we place the Magician alongside in order to thus study his fourth step. The Magician seems to wish to pass straight into the chamber of the dead in order to pass across the threshold. It seems as if he had never had any other wish. Yet we will see that the Way indeed passes not only over this threshold but moves onwards as well.

These are the interpretative factors provided by this card:

the end of a development;
conclusion as a new start;
the end of an illusion (manifest nowadays as disillusionment);
the courage to integrate oneself into the cycle of life;
pride in what is completed, now to be rewarded;
efforts until the end in this life;
the way into the afterlife;
journey across the great heavenly ocean.

The goddess of death, by the way, looks rightward, indicating the future. It is significant that she looks to the side, for death should not be cruel to look at (as on many misunderstood cards XIII from other games of tarot), for death is finally nothing other than the signpost to the future.

With the fourth step of the Magician we have now reached the fifth stage of the Way of Osiris. It was Osiris himself who exemplified this transition in his own life after he had been murdered by his brother Seth and cut into pieces. His Serket was Isis who collected all the pieces of Osiris which had been spread to the four winds, then put them together and then conceived from the deceased - as if from another world - the child Horus, to whom she then gave the light of the world. The Way of Osiris then leads back into one's own experiences, being only an example, just as everything divine should be exemplary. The people who have grasped this are already far advanced on the way of initiation; they have understood something of what awaits them. And that depends upon what they have performed or achieved in the "past" world. Now the seeker, the Magician, is next entering the presence of the Great Deity who teaches him the measure of all things.

XIV.   THE
        TWO URNS

Number:

XIV

Transformation of the staff:

THE RAY OF ETERNITY

Motto:

THE MEASURE IS THE MEASURE

XIV. The Two Urns

The first look reveals a colossal statue which nevertheless appears strangely alive. In the background on the right you can see stars of the firmament, on the other side a heavenly body that could be either sun or moon. From the earth the sun and moon look roughly of equal size (if we take the full moon), although the moon is in fact far smaller. But the proximity of the moon to the earth offsets the relationship in size. The diameter of the sun is four hundred times greater than that of the moon, but in compensation the moon is four hundred times nearer to the earth than the sun. Thus both seem to be of equal size. This approximate relation is to be transferred in principle to the difference between deity and man, though it is here not a matter of the ratio of four hundred to one, which is merely a symbolic comparison.

Behind the colossal statue of the deity the Milky Way has been passing by, while in front of the statue you can see - disproportionately smaller - the seeker standing, still on his way towards initiation. Having put the experience of the Threshold behind him, he is now looking straight ahead, for the first time in harmony with the deity, into the face of the observer.

Since card XII 'The Hanging One' the outward appearance of the seeker has seemed to be simpler. The clothing has been reduced to a minimum; it no longer depends on 'covering' garments, any disguise. It is also not important which god we are dealing with here. Whoever scrutinizes the face of the statue a bit more closely will realize that at least two gods can be discerned, since the dark image is supplemented by the light one. For each of these two deities there is a flower with seven blossoms reaching up towards the heavens, just as two streams are being poured from the larger urn into the smaller one. They might be streams of holy water of which no drop may be lost, or it could be a matter of light beams or some other mental or spiritual flow. In any case it is a gift of the gods which produces some fruitful impact on mankind. This gift is only apportioned to people who have found the correct proportions for themselves. This is one of the hardest tasks which have to be solved during our lives, but whoever solves it for himself will neither suffer from inferiority complexes nor be at risk of pride or arrogance.

This measure is not the polarity which has been so frequently addressed. In fact it is really a question about the right assessment of relations and measures, for heaven is not the same as earth, human not equal to divine, servant not equal to a ruler; or, as the Greeks knew: what is permitted to Jupiter is far from being allowed to the ox. The beginner is not equivalent to the teacher, initiate to the adept, even though the one can become the other. With one exception: man can never become equal to God; he can only attempt to come close to God in order to gain his blessing.

It is necessary to learn at this stage of the initiation process that, while there are complementary opposites, there are also contrasts which are not of equal value. Here each one has to find his own yardstick or measuring unit for himself, something demanding an intensive self-examination and self-criticism. Yet without doing so no-one can be an example to others and certainly not an initiated adept. Speaking and keeping silent are polar opposites, but speaking and remaining quiet can - from the viewpoint of value - be quite different in themselves. Question and answer are complementary but this says nothing about the content of a question or an answer. Caution is not cowardice, but may lead to it; but caution can be courageous. The alchemists - and there were such people among the ancient Egyptians - had to learn with all consequences that lead is not the same as lead, just as gold does not have to be the same as gold.

The initiated, as well as all those who assess, judge or lead, have to learn to distinguish, to find the right yardstick at the right time for the particular matter or situation; though here it is not a question of good and evil, for the Scales of Conscience lie behind us. It us about finding the right measure or standard in order to set standards.

The original measure of all things, namely the measurement of time and rhythms, was provided by the heavens, and the study of the stars - not astronomy here - is based on this, for with this heavenly scale people have become able to grasp and to measure. This is, however, only true for the basic disposition of a person - not for the development. The measure for this must be set by everyone for himself, and according to that he will be judged one day. And such a yardstick must also be valid for his personal relation of expectation and performance, from wanting and doing, from wishing and giving. Whoever, for example, judges others must first of all reveal what standard he has set himself for self-assessment, before he dares to approach others with his opinion. If he does not find the measuring standard within himself, if he does not apply a higher standard to himself, he has reached a pre-judgement, that is created a prejudice. Therefore the measurement of the self is the standard par excellence with which others are allowed to judge us, before we judge others ourselves. This is ancient divine teaching which is found in all religions, but was particularly taught in the temples of the Egyptians.

The symbol (of an external nature) for the perfect yardstick is demonstrated by the pyramid of Cheops; it cannot be improved on from the viewpoint of measurement ratios. This construction was to be constructed, according to human standards, for eternity. This standard was achieved from the human viewpoint at the time of those constructing it, but for the gods 5000 years are maybe but a breath. Who knows? We do not know the divine measuring unit, just as we also do not know the measure between the two urns at the fifteenth step of the Magician. Yet the urns lead us to suppose (as expressed by the proverb) that the gods leave us when the measure is full. That's what it is about.

If we place the Magician alongside this card, we can see at a glance how small the Magician has become - and at the same time how sublime. God does not give in order to receive, but humans have to give if they wish to receive something back - that too is a unit of measure.

Now to the factors for interpreting this card:

> *inner justice;*
> *recognition of one's own possibilities;*
> *the measure for oneself in this world;*
> *inner balance;*
> *harmony with the world;*
> *love in faith;*
> *acknowledgement of the differences.*

We have also reached the fifth stage of the Way of Isis, in which the relation of the two urns should be of great importance, for - as all beloved goddesses - Isis was (mis) appropriated by believers, one could even say made human. We have been aware of this ever since we have used the name of the

Mother of God, Mary, so frequently as a first name (for women and even for men), so the divine-ness of this name has been lost.

Although children were baptized at first in the name of the mother of God, people had not taken the proportional measure into consideration. The way we are familiar with in our own times does not seem to have been the same in Egypt; however, numerous queen pharaohs or other leading daughters of pharaohs added the name of Isis as an epithet to their state goddesses, whose representatives they felt themselves to be. And this was true for all deities in ancient Egypt. The dissolution of belief had thus already set in, although that would have been hardly noticed by the simple believer.

Yet how does it help when the measuring standard of the Two Urns is not acknowledged or has been forgotten? What impact this has will be evident in the following card.

Number:

XV

Transformation of the staff:

THE TORCH

Motto:

SEARCHING AS ADDICTION BECOMES TEMPTATION

XV. DEMON

A t first glance we can see a part-human, part-animal figure appearing like the stylized god-dog Seth, who entered ancient Egyptian mythology as a villain because he deceived his brother Osiris, then killed him and cut him into pieces. Seth thus became the great adversary of Osiris, just as the Devil or Satan became the antagonist to the Christian God. Both, however, whether Seth or the Devil (that was not a term familiar to the Egyptians, by the way, which is why the card is called Demon) were once gods with the task of bringing light to mankind. Lucifer, bringer of light, tried to tempt mankind by persuading them as follows: if you accept my light, you will be like gods. That was his sin.

Seth on the other hand did not begrudge Osiris for bringing the light; Seth considered himself to be the true bringer of light. This was in fact with some justification, for his star, the dog star, rises in summer = when the Nile floods and inundations came - shortly before the sun, i.e. before the onset of light. The dog star, Sirius, was the star according to which the whole Egyptian calendar was oriented. This star in the constellation Canis Major or Big Dog was that of the god Seth. Seth was the herald of light, but not the light itself, the sun. However, he was never able to tolerate this fact - according to Egyptian mythology. He wished to be the first among the gods, but he had to eliminate his brother first to achieve this aim. This would have succeeded without the intervention of Isis. Due to this, his image got distorted to the extent of being depicted as the devilish and ugly demon that unites all the characteristics of evil within it. Yet the strength of Seth as adversary should never be underestimated.

The power of the Demon is revealed in the promises and temptations that he makes and dangles in front of seekers, for instance, the power to put themselves in the place of a deity or to promise those who are not seeking instead a paradise on earth, in which they should enjoy their sensuality to the full.

This can be clearly seen in the picture. The seeker is not portrayed here but instead some kind of allegorical man and woman. The man and the woman are in the claws of the demon. They seem to be bound to one another, cannot apparently escape from each other. The flowers are clearly growing well above the bodies of the sitting couple who have given themselves to their natural drives and appetites. They are being watched and goaded on by a snake which extends itself from the demon's belt. The demon pays no attention whatsoever to them, for he is concerned with the seekers whom he in fact wishes to lead into temptation. To them he promises the light of heaven which he has obtained direct from the sun with his torch. With this, however, he is indicating seekers the way into the future (to the right of the observer); thus he can be addressed - adapted from Goethe's Faust - as "the spirit that desires evil but creates good".

The demon is on his way, desiring to show us what his light is capable of doing. Seth, for instance, knew that the family of the gods had to stick together. Thus he protected the sungod while the latter, reaching out of the sun barque (moon crescent), was stabbing Apophis, the snake of the underworld, to death with a lance.

At this stage the magnificent mythology of the Egyptians comes to the fore once again, a mythology acknowledging neither eternally good nor absolute evil. There is always a struggle in order to conserve what exists already and to make every development towards a higher being possible. The demon is particularly dangerous for those who seek something without enough patience and lose their composure when they do not find what they were seeking quickly enough and cannot take it for themselves. That is the issue in this phase of the way to initiation, when the ambiguously evil element in the Demon encounters us.

In the service of Seth, the demon is always taking up the struggle against Osiris. As he himself cannot harm Osiris, he tries to prevent those desiring to reach Osiris from taking this path, sets traps for them, or even attempts to get them to rebel against Osiris. The demon had one particular speciality - if we may use this term here - such that he thought he could get all magicians to force the gods to act according to his wishes. With this promise he tempted many seekers to find what they were seeking more quickly. He had tricks and wizardry at his disposal in order to present examples for his magic powers. This is where the truly demonic in the temptations lay, which many seekers could not draw back from.

This sixth step on the Magician's Way can be examined in greater depth if we lay card I alongside. We can see clearly that the Magician takes pleasure in his magic equipment and maybe he is impatient to use his instruments. This is where any demons - or whoever - can start playing various powers against each other. The ibis on card I warns us that we have time enough; but how gladly such warnings, quietly expressed, remain simply unnoticed, when the sunbird is calling, as it flies above the star that appears so full of promise to the Magician. The Magician, like all seekers, is very much at risk when it is a matter of being told about a rapid fulfillment of his wishes. Such danger is pre-eminent and still greater than the danger which arises from sensual desires, even though enough people, that have set out on the way of initiation, have stumbled due to that too. What it is really all about is the viewpoint of far-sightedness or short-sightedness. The pair that the Demon has in its claws cannot see beyond the partner, is short-sighted; just as is the one that thinks he is going to reach the destination quickly. The latter seems more dangerous because the sensual orgy can quickly evaporate, whereas turning away from the real goal means the end for those who have set out on the path of higher knowledge; for they have been enjoined not to fall for the demon. Just as all prophets, seers and ascetics fall into temptation, the seekers, too, who have set out on the way of initiation, do not only have to avoid the Demon but also to courageously withstand its artifices.

This results in the following interpretation factors:

appetites;
desire;
temptation;
impatience;
the wish to be god-like;
black magic;
the anti-god;
the revolutionary.

The Way of Horus represents, among the three ways of the deities that have been examined so far, the most human way. For it is here that the degree of susceptibility to human desires is tested and where it is determined whether this is the quick satisfaction of desires or the attempt to be god-like. The Demon we encounter here does not have to be sought outside; it lives within us, it has come into the world with us, it has grown with us. That is the great concern of the soul: to overcome this demon at some point. Here humans are left to themselves. There is no divine help. The gods expect human beings to do this work themselves. If this has been understood we can move on to the next card.

Number:
XVI

Transformation of the staff:
THE LIGHTNING FLASH

Motto:
STANDSTILL WOULD BE THE END

XVI. THE TOWER

A first glance shows us an awesome flash of lightning cast down from an udjat eye (eye of God) and striking a large building. The building is the entrance to a temple, a so-called pylon. Two people are hurled off the pylon; they are tumbling head downwards and losing the masks which they had been wearing over their faces. A storm has arrived, as can be seen by the eight flowers straining on either side. The pylon has burst asunder.

The udjat eye was a symbol for the god of the heavens, Horus, who thus kept his eye on human beings. This udjat eye was understood by people to be a sacred sign and so became a popular amulet, hardly less popular indeed than the scarab. 'The eye of Horus' was considered to be most vigilant. One eye always represents the sun, the other the moon. If the sun, which had brought everything to the light of day, now saw that something had developed on earth which did not please the gods, then bolts of lightning were cast down to warn people and, if necessary, to punish them. Flashes of lightning were concentrated rays of the sun according to how primitive peoples imagined them; they were welded together in the smithy of the gods when the heavens darkened, in order then to be cast down onto the earth. Thunderstorms often arise around the Mediterranean quite quickly, so people are taken by surprise again and again. Thus thunder and lightning felt terrifying and were seen as a punishment of the gods.

According to spiritual and medical experience (and the Egyptians were masters in both fields), what threatened a person, also protected them. Thus the eye of Horus, which the latter had lost in his battle with Seth, was not only worn as an amulet but above all decorated the coffins, the 'false' doors to the tombs; and it was also worn on each 'pectoral' breastplate. Incidentally, it was the god Thoth, lord of time, who once again inserted the lost eye back in its socket for Horus. That is maybe where the saying from folk wisdom originates that time heals all wounds. This udjat eye was fixed onto coffins because there was a general conviction that the dead could look through these eyes in order to view the external world and observe how their own family members cared for the dead. Since they were already in the realms of heaven, the dead could - similarly to the gods - punish people.

People felt safe from punishment in the temple. That is why they often barricaded themselves behind the first pylon. Only the highest ranking priests were permitted to enter the holy of holies. Behind the pylon there was mostly a large courtyard with statues of the gods and pillared halls. People could spend time here. The pylon on our card is only a symbol, however; it is intended to express that the people, having conquered the demons in themselves, have withdrawn into their own temple.

However, the struggle is very strenuous and tiring, so people have a need of peace and quiet; they believe that they have now achieved enough. This has to lead to an inner crustification. Nothing could be more mistaken than to stand still, to stop for a pause: resting which leads to 'rusting'. That is why the gods send down bolts of lightening to drive people onwards, to tear people's masks off their faces. The gods deny them the safe haven behind which they have barricaded themselves so that they can continue the Way - perhaps through necessity rather than willingly. Here the gods actively intervene on the Way of Initiation in order to guide those who have penetrated so far onwards.

The assistance of the gods can be hoped for. That does not mean, however, that the gods allow us to receive any benefits here, that they even reward our deficiencies! On the contrary: benefaction can also consist of punishments since most of us only react to strokes of fate which demand something of us. The Greeks expressed this still more clearly, since their highest god, Zeus, who showed a certain similarity with Osiris, punished one thing above all: ingratitude. Whoever leans back with relief and pleasure, whoever does not strive onwards, whoever does not wish to create something from his gifts, whoever leaves talents neglected or misuses them, such a person was always seen from the view of Olympus as highly ungrateful and had to be punished.

Whoever shuts himself off, walls himself away, believes he has made it, barricades himself in order not to have to make sacrifices for others, whoever does not encourage anyone, does not teach, such a person brings down the anger of the gods upon himself. And these gods punish figuratively with thunder and lightening; then punishment strikes like a bolt of lightening into a person's life, then threatening clouds gather, even though the world around may be bathed in brilliant sunlight. Thunderstorms come unannounced; as a rule we are not prepared for them, and when they do come, everyone believes the bolt will not strike them. That is why the people are surprised, as in this picture, since they have been cast down virtually naked. They could have run out of the entrance of their pylon, for the door is not closed. But no, they had hidden themselves away on the towers, had believed they could hide from the anger of the gods, like children who go into a corner and believe that seeing no-one, they remain unseen. Yet it is just those people who wish to go on, aspiring to initiation, who have to realize that the eye of god looks everywhere, because this eye resides in fact in everyone of us. It is within us; God, the creator, looks out from within. Every person is his eye! That is the decisive insight which can be gained on this seventh stage of the Magician.

For a deeper view of this card we lay the magician's card alongside. The Magician stands there at the beginning with his hands full - and now? He has had to give up everything because he was already convinced that he had reached his goal by overcoming his demons. If he did not have the inner knowledge already, he would have to start again from the very beginning. But the inner knowledge is available; the magic instruments are no longer needed from now onwards. The bolt of lightening has to strike just so that people can realize this fact: that there is a milestone on the Way, after which nothing external is needed any longer, after which it is only a matter of knowledge, insight, ability and maybe of wisdom.

The interpretation factors for this card are consequently:

the lightning bolt;
being startled or scared;
awakening from torpor;
an end to crustification;
the warning punishment;
being torn out of one's dreams;
sudden event;
the unpredictable;
sudden ruin.

An important factor represented by this stage includes the need for people to give up their over-dependence on the head or mind. That is why they fall with their head downwards in the picture, indeed no longer downwards of their own free will, as with the Hanging One. Here there is nothing happening according to one's own free will; that is the significant difference.

For the Osiris Way this is the sixth step since this god could also reveal himself to be an angry one, exhorting and admonishing. This should indicate that it is not enough to rely on the gods alone; every act of benevolence and mercy has to be earned and every gift must be paid for; no-one can rely on eternal good fortune. Even Osiris had to experience this once and divine experience has to serve as an example for man. Osiris let himself be tricked, Seth thereby gaining power over him. What would then have developed out of the family of gods and of men, just because one deity had not been alert enough? Nowadays our image is maybe of those sitting in ivory towers not knowing what goes on around them.

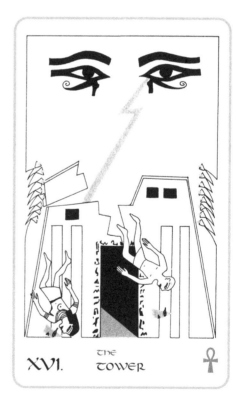

XVII. THE MAGIC STAR

Number:

XVII

Transformation of the staff:

THE HEAVENLY NILE

Motto:

MAGIC IS LOVE — LOVE IS MAGIC

XVII. The Magic Star

A first look reveals a woman on a lotus blossom. Her hands make the link between the heavenly Nile (the Milky Way) and the flowers of this world, showing seventeen blooms in total. The lotus blossom is like a chalice, but also like a throne. The woman, perhaps a priestess of Isis, is sitting with her legs folded and with a proud posture on her throne of flowers. She is richly decorated and festively clothed. Her face is friendly but has something supernatural about it. On her head she is wearing the symbol of sun and moon in one. It is the (stylized) moon barque which, like a ship, transports the sun through the night. However, we can also recognise in this head decoration the symbol of the Apis bull, the two bull's horns through which the sun passes. Both forms of the moon's appearance as a crescent are meant with this symbol, namely the waning or dying moon and the waxing or new-born moon.

Over the whole picture shines the magic star, with its eight rays of light. The luminary Venus was always seen as having eight rays, since Venus appears in the evening sky until the waxing moon crescent passes by her eight times. Then Venus becomes the morning star and shines until the dying moon has also passed by her eight times. In this way the number eight became the number of Venus, also expressed in the cross total of card XVII (card 17 = 1+7 = 8) from a numerological viewpoint.

It is a peaceful picture full of charm and inner, quiet power. One feels that Isis rules here; this is her realm, from which the power of love and magic spreads out into the whole world, indeed is intended to radiate in this way.

The Magic Star floats above this peaceful atmosphere. Today we call this star the planet Venus, though earlier it may even have been called Isis (this can no longer be established). Venus, as morning or as evening star (both are impossible simultaneously on one day or rather in one night), shines with a soft and harmonious light. This luminary shines only during the evening or morning, not during the middle of the night. In the evening Venus illuminates just a touch more impressively in the increasing darkness than in the morning because the sun gradually appears in the dawn and the morning star is then quickly absorbed into the red of sunrise. These two 'stars', which are one luminary, but are always separated in their appearances, were also related to different deities. Thus the morning star was assigned to the martial death-bringing lion goddess Sekhmet, whereas the softer evening star was seen as relating to Bastet the gentler cat goddess.

Overall, however, Venus was associated with Isis. It taught people through its luminosity in early times that there were heavenly bodies other than the fixed stars, in fact planets, for Venus took its own path (as did the others planets). However, this fact was most obvious and notable with Venus. That is why she also received the name of the magic star. With this planet we might say arose the lore of the stars, astrology, even though Isis/Venus is not a real star at all, but a dark mass (planet), which only reflects sunlight, as do the other planets. Yet Venus is able to shine so brightly and luminously in Egypt that the headings of newspapers can be easily read by its light. This star then provides some real illumination in the twilight before the moon has risen.

This magic star was the reason as previously mentioned that people began to occupy themselves more intensively with celestial laws, for previously the great priests and astrologers had been largely concerned with the rhythms of sun and moon, and otherwise all calculations were based on the pole or north star. The Cheops pyramid was aligned to it, whereby the southern sun gained a counter-pole in the north.

Thus this 'magic star' assisted man in recognizing and recording the celestial laws and in learning to submit to them; for in the heavens harmony ruled, reliability and deep peace, even though everything constantly changed in the heavens. Basically, however, despite this constant change, everything remained as a pattern, with a steady development based on constant principles.

Heavenly peace was also sought on earth by mankind. The star sometimes became associated with being a 'companion through the night' since it shone in the evening when the darkness fell and shone again in the morning when the dawn began to show (though never both in the same night, just to anticipate the scientific arguments of astronomers). For the same reason, Isis/Venus was also called the lovers' star, since young lovers sometimes met by the light of this star in the evenings and at other times separated early in the dawn twilight, seeing its light before the day's toils began.

Egypt was familiar with many love goddesses. Apart from Isis there was Hathor in particular. Isis was the symbol of love for all, the good one reigning over all; Hathor was the goddess of personal feelings and relationships. Much of her cult was later transferred to the Greek Aphrodite. Into her were projected all the birthing, nursing, protecting powers of women. Thus the woman on the lotus also symbolizes something of the Hathor priestesses, particularly as Horus was often seen as her spouse.

Hathor's son was 'Ihi', god of music. This Magic Star then was also associated with the arts, indeed everything beautiful and sublime. Ihi was able to create miracles, as could Isis, who possessed the ability to place children in the fire night by night to ensure their immortality, just as she had fanned the breath of life into Osiris once more.

In this card XVII, the Magic Star, (and thus in the priestess herself) we can say that several female deities offering blessings have been combined into a single focus. Isis in first place, but also the beautiful cow-eyed Hathor, as well as the lion goddess Sekhmet and the cat-faced Bastet. This leads us to the following interpretations:

love;
beauty;
symmetry;
peace;
the arts;
music;
the muses;
heavenly and earthly bonds;
deep happiness and content;
the harmony of life;
the beauty of nature.

If we place the Magician's card alongside it, we can then see (and this is the reason for doing so only after having summarized the interpretation factors) that the priestess of multiple identities is showing him the way beyond himself. He is not permitted to stay with her for long, he has to assimilate her. He can rest here but his way is not finished; he has to go on, the search has to continue. Many may wish what Goethe so splendidly expressed: 'if I should say to you this moment, bide with me, you are so beautiful, then you may put me in chains, for then I am gladly willing to face my ruin!'

Yet this is not the final conclusion of wisdom, as Faust was forced to realize and to learn. Beauty is never alone the goal! We have reached the sixth, the penultimate stage of the Way of Isis, are able to understand Isis in her beauty and in her mercy - in contrast to the sixth stage of the Way of Osiris, in which this god was angry. It is as if Isis wishes to offset what Osiris believed he had to do; yet the result of this might be expressed as: 'if you follow Osiris, then you can also become more aware through me of the harmony of the worlds and the interconnection of the cosmos and the earth.' For the Milky Way of the Heavenly Nile was according to Egyptian thinking also the celestial Tree of Life, towards which every person strove in order to be able to live eternally in the realm of the stars.

1. THE
MAGICIAN

XVII. THE
MAGIC STAR

XVIII. THE MOON

Number:

XVIII

Transformation of the staff:

THE WAY

Motto:

THE GOAL IS THE LIGHT AND THE DARK

95

XVIII. THE MOON

A first glance reveals a path leading up towards the heavens, to the sun and the moon, to the waxing and waning lunar crescent, to the stars. The sun may be eclipsed (by the earth's shadow), the moon turns into a dark moon and the stars disappear behind clouds. Yet sun, moon and stars retain their luminescence; they keep their signpost function, so that humans can align themselves by these signs and strive to reach them. At this stage of initiation there is a change of direction. If the future, the goal, has only lain to the right up to the present, now the Way lies upwards, past two pyramids and two Anubis dogs.

The Way (apparently) begins between two (stylized) flowering shrubs, each with nine blossoms. And the symbolic creature which carries the sun through the night, through the realm of darkness - namely the scarab or dung-beetle - has started out on this Way so that the light may return at dawn.

The scarab is the symbol of life par excellence. It accompanies the dead, just as it does when shoving the sun through the night in front of it. The beetle - a creature zoologically treated as a low life form - becomes the symbol of heaven, the symbol of reincarnation. This range within Egyptian mysticism, Egyptian religions and esotericism, is so overwhelming that one can only observe it full of awe and absorb this awareness within us. There was no pharaoh, no priest, no citizen who did not have a scarab placed in their death shrine or tomb.

For the living this scarab served as an amulet, for the dead as a guide through the night towards the other shore. In nature the dung beetle rolls its eggs into a ball of dung such that the young beetles evidently emerge without procreation, as if by themselves. Just like the young dung beetles, the sun god appeared morning after morning, without procreation, as the self-created original godhead.

In this way the scarab accompanies the seeker up to the heights, into the inner sanctuary, in order to receive the final initiation. This way to the heights, into the sanctuary, can take place during the day or in the course of the night. To decide this is alone a matter for the gods, not for the seeker. Yet everyone can follow the way of the scarab; this is also ancient knowledge. It is a new way for those who take it and a very distant way, which might require a number of lives. Yet this fact does not play any real role, for even Osiris had to be freed by Isis several times, not only after he had been cut into pieces by Seth. He had already once been in Seth's trap, Seth having created a coffin which was to belong to the person who fitted into it as if tailor-made for them. Isis lay down in the coffin; her sister and others tried it out too, but when Osiris lay down in the coffin and he fitted to the millimeter, Seth suddenly closed the coffin and tipped it into the Nile. The coffin floated far out into the sea and beached on the coast of Palestine. There it remained and was completely absorbed into the growing trunk of a tree, until it could no longer be seen. Yet Isis found the coffin, which had meanwhile been serving as a pillar of wood in a palace, and was able to free Osiris.

The Way may be long, but the goal will be reached as long as it is consequentially followed. That of course requires discipline, which is made clear in this case by the two Anubis dogs; not only the light external aspect of the dogs is disciplined but the dark internal aspect must be so too. Only the whole leads to initiation, the whole must be striving towards heaven, even if this should lie in an earthly domain.

It is the ninth stage of the Way of the Magician who no longer seems to be present, for if we place card number I alongside this picture, then we can realize first of all what a long way the Magician has travelled, even if he still seems far from having reached his goal.

The Magician is out of place in this picture; he can only feel himself to be the scarab symbolically or entrust himself to it; then he knows that the way he has taken is the right one. The outward appearance of the human being is no longer needed; here not even depictions of the gods are required any longer. It is enough to recognise the two pyramids. Pyramids were also burial chambers, but in the first instance they were places of initiation, for there was an atmosphere inside them which enabled a person to take up the streams and currents of the universe such that the spirit could rise up to become aware of new dimensions. In the pyramids there lived the spirit which had gone far beyond earthly thought, even though this spirit may not yet be the spirit of the gods. However, the latter divine power should not be fully absorbed by any human being. A human can never become a god, he can only approach this state, getting close in order to receive his blessings. This largely occurred in sanctuaries and other holy places at first, and later in the pyramids.

The god of the rising sun is called Chepre (after the dung beetle) and is often depicted with a scarab head. Chepre holds the ruler's scepter and the ankh cross in its hands. The scarab also links the seeker with the gods, is thus the one whose way has to be followed, however far it may lead.

Thus we come to the following factors for the interpretation of card XVIII:

starting out from the depths;
the distant goal;
the great decision (in contrast to card VI);
inner discipline;
the acceptance of light and dark as being of equal value, as complementary factors;
belief in the final goal.

The card is called 'The Moon' because in ancient Egypt the moon had already become the symbol of the heavens representing the hope of constant renewal. For it must have always affected people incredibly when they repeatedly experienced how something visibly dies and visibly resurrects once again. Nowadays this inner 'way of the moon' is hardly accepted any more because the soul has been largely rejected by scientists as unprovable. Yet love is not an objectively provable phenomenon either, though fortunately people still experience it today, despite the fact that provability in a scientific sense controls our thinking. The Egyptians knew about everything which is dismissed nowadays as 'belief', even as 'superstition' - a concept which did not exist in those times, out of respect for the convictions of other people.

We have arrived at the sixth stage of the Way of Horus. Man sets out on his way towards the deity, thus leaving his early path, at least as far as the mental level is concerned. He wants to be near his deity, his soul, his depths.

1. THE MAGICIAN

XVIII. THE MOON

XIX.   THE SUN

Number:

XIX

Transformation of the staff:

THE TREE

Motto:

FEMININE IS FOUND IN MASCULINE, MASCULINE IN FEMININE

XIX. THE SUN

The first glance sees a young couple (the emphasis not being on young) holding hands in front of a tree with nineteen blossoms. The sun shines directly overhead while below flowers have formed a lemniscate. Peace reigns and both people are looking at each other happily; each one needs the other. The woman is looking in the direction of the future, the man towards the past, but both are standing in the present. The highest happiness of the present moment is the joy of union, the happiness that links two people, the joy of love.

Love is also initiation! There is no initiation without love. There are indeed many books and traditions which state that the initiated should do without the happiness of love in order to concentrate on the highest thing, but the greatest joy in the present is the link in which two opposites come together and the heavenly marriage takes place. For without the bodies which are born through a connection, there would be no more space for the development of a soul in this world. In the here and now the seeker experiences that happiness is present, has to be present. For initiation also has to take place so that happiness on earth may be protected by the initiation itself, since it is the striving for good fortune or happiness which first motivated us to set out on the path to initiation.

The tree is a decisive element in the picture. The tree growing up towards the heavens is the symbol of the earth. But a tree can only grow as high as its roots permit. If it loses the power of its roots, it topples and the struggle for upward growth comes to a permanent end. Once a tree has fallen, it can no longer be set up again, unless it is a very young tree which can still be 'raised'.

No effort leading away from this earth is of use to us. Whoever wishes to enter the initiation heaven without considering what he has to do here below, will fly away into distances which are infinite, but which do not permit any return to earth.

The picture of the tree was always manifest in the heavens too. That means of course the Milky Way which the Egyptians called the heavenly Nile. In the northern hemisphere you can see both branches of the tree in the summer, in the winter the trunk. The priestly astrologers were thus also able to determine the passing of the seasons based on the Milky Way: from the trunk to life (both branches on which the fruit ripens), from life to the trunk again.

This tree in the heavens is also the tree in which Osiris lived on in his coffin, the one in which his hostile brother, Seth, held him captive. Isis was forced to search for him in heaven and on earth. Thus every tree had something to do with the breath of Osiris. Osiris lives in every tree; and to be one with the blessing of Osiris was once the yearning of all people: the lovers, the faithful, the seekers, the doubters, the happy as well as the unfortunate. In the tree there seems to be endless life force, unless human beings take it from the tree.

Above all, one must not forget the sun! If it is shining, you can no longer see the tree of heaven, the heavenly Nile, the Milky Way; yet sunshine does earthly trees a power of good; without it they would not be able to flourish.

The earthly tree symbolizes the secret of life during the day as well, namely the light and the dark in one. The tree provides shade, as we say today; but once the view was held that trees reminded us of the dark also during the day, for it was precisely in regions where the sun's heat is destructive that a longing emerged for the dark and for the shadowy.

The tree alone - before temples and other buildings were erected - provided this shade, and in the woods it was easiest of all to flee from this 'only brightness'. No wonder most fairy tales and legends in this world assume that secret powers are found in woods and forests, that elves and gnomes, beings with supernatural powers, are at home there because this is where they flourish best and where they can hide most easily. The evil spirits reside in the hills and mountains which is why they have to emerge from the mountain to visit the human world.

The tree expresses - in a symbolic and a real sense - the contrasts of this world. The striving to reach the light, but also the being imprisoned in darkness, the brightness and the shadow, the heat and the coolness, the power of growth and the knowledge about limitations, for no tree grows into the heavens.

Lovers also used to meet beneath the palms of the oases in Egypt, for the heat of the open desert would singe each and every love. What offered shade was taken from the palm fronds which later provided a model for designing fans.

It has already been indicated that the Magician is no longer really present here, but he has taken on the good fortune which the Magic Star (XVII) has shown him, after which he has then started on the great Way of the scarab. His Way has not yet ended, even if the early happiness - also in the higher sense - of everlasting love has seemingly been reached. For love which links people eternally lives; and it is not without reason that we know that the souls of these people encounter each other again, that they live through and have to master new experiences together on the ladder upwards.

It is the last stage for the Magician, whose Way ends here. A more beautiful goal and end cannot be imagined; that is the gift of Osiris, whose Way has also reached its seventh and final stage here. Osiris and the Magician stretch out their hands to each other, have become in fact one - of course only seen from the viewpoint of the Magician.

We can now summarize the factors arising out of the interpretation of card XIX:

> *growth through union of masculine and feminine;*
> *balance of light and shadow;*
> *valuing of opposites in self;*
> *harmony of past and future in present;*
> *love as a state of mutual respect and shared energies;*
> *well-rooted in earth to reach the heavens;*
> *vitality by achieving harmony within the self.*

Osiris, according to Egyptian mythology, the eldest son of the goddess of the heavens, Nut, who we still have to encounter, and the earth god, Geb. Out of the relationship between heaven and earth he ascends to the position of highest god among the gods. With this it becomes clear that heaven and earth must always be seen as a totality, that heaven marries earth in a human sense in order to thus develop towards the act of creation. This is the secret which also encapsulates the belief that the earthly cannot simply be laid aside. Whoever believes this has not understood the sense of initiation, because heaven and earth are meant to be united and the earth may not be misused as a springboard for attaining heaven. This world and the other are one, and whatever ascends from the earth, has to return to the earth, and whatever descends from heaven, ascends to heaven once again to bring joy to the earth in eternal interplay. For however much heaven may be angered, it still loves the earth.

1. THE
    MAGICIAN

XIX. THE
      SUN

XX. RESURRECTION

Number:

XX

Transformation of the staff:

The Instrument of heaven

Motto:

Initiation is worth striving for, so the soul will cope in heaven

XX. RESURRECTION

A first look reveals the burial chamber of an ancient Egyptian grave made in some cavern. Above, stars and constellations have been painted to form the heavens. We can see Taurus, Leo and the Pole Star at the end of Leo's tail. The original motifs of these first stylized constellations (not zodiac signs) are found in the golden hall of the royal burial chamber of Sethos I.

It is no coincidence that we find ourselves, at the end of the way, in a tomb built for a king who called himself after the 'villain' Seth, i.e. after the Demon. At the end of any 'Way' good and bad are united, for both are stages on a path of initiation, during which we have to overcome the bad and are not permitted to misuse the good. At the left side of the picture we see twenty blooms in three bundles, and next to them three resurrection stages of a mummy. From above the heavenly trumpet extends down into the picture, exhorting the dead to get ready for departure. (Later it was said that it called the dead to the last judgement, but the Great Judgement, the Scales of Conscience, already lay for the dead in Egypt behind them at this point in time.)

Thus after the card of the golden Sun follows the card of the dark tomb, showing that both have to be united. Yet this card does not have a dark or dismal impact but is more joyful and constructive, almost optimistic and encouraging.

The tomb - whether that of a king or of any other citizen - was never a dismal or depressing place. The dead received amulets, useful tools and also victuals placed in the grave for their long journey. That was not all, however; literature was also given for them to take. We are aware of many texts that were later published in the Egyptian books of the dead. The tombs were painted. These paintings - however visually appealing they may be - were never intended for observers, but just for the dead who had started on their long journey.

Many of the texts given to the dead to take with them represented magic explanations for the life on the other side. There was a really small, restricted section of the priesthood that passed on the secret knowledge orally to the living, but wrote it down for the dead to take with them. The final secret, however, was never written down where any living person could read it.

The final secret is anyway one that is more to be sensed, divined, than really known; the wise were convinced that this knowledge would be breathed into the initiated by their soul when the soul itself considered it to be the right time. This was then the last sign of initiation, the highest distinction that anyone could achieve. The most important explanations were also not written on the walls of the tombs but on the insides, and sometimes outsides, of the coffins. They were also messages to those who had already reached the other shore.

All these texts were later summarized in the various 'Books of the Gates, the Caverns, the Day and the Night' and many other writings. But the inner connection is missing in these works, and much sounds - as might be expected - as if most items have been torn out of their context. The overall connection would probably only have been comprehensible to the highest sages, who had already departed from the earth, however, when people re-discovered the sense of the texts of coffins and tombs.

The Egyptians were fully convinced that initiation could only be truly completed when the seeker experienced death in a conscious condition, so to say anticipated it. The encounter with crossing the threshold was the last and decisive test. Nowadays the general opinion is that initiation ceremonies were undertaken in the larger and smaller pyramids.

Whoever visits the Cheops pyramid sees the remains of a sarcophagus made of granite in the royal chamber. That is where the seekers - before receiving the last consecration rites of initiation - are said to have been placed in, indeed according to the example of Osiris, with the lid of the coffin closed. The hours of this burial alive must have been terrible, especially because the seekers never had any assurance that they would be resurrected again. This was left to the deity. Many seekers indeed knew people who were initiated, but they never experienced if all who had been placed in a closed coffin also emerged from it again, whether a heavenly instrument called them to rise up again. That the embalmed mummies did not rise again could be realistically followed by the Egyptians in the course of time, but this did not prevent them from doubting the resurrection of the essential elements of the living in corporeal form.

In order to master this trial, an inner connection with Isis was absolutely necessary, for only confidence in her powers of bringing the dead back to life gave someone the strength to entrust themselves to the stone coffin.

We have also arrived at the seventh stage of the Way of Isis. At this point it is a good idea to lay the picture of the High Priestess alongside the card 'Resurrection', for this is the first step (of two) of the High Priestess. And it is noticeable that the staff the priestess holds in her hand and which seems all-powerful to us, has in fact been transformed into the instrument of heaven. The High Priestess calls, then; she is the one who judges who is initiated, who not, or who needs more time. While lying in the closed coffin the seekers are visited by any monsters and demons that are still inside them, just as their whole life also unrolls before their inner eye. Many people can bear this because they experience how they find themselves taking the role of Ma'at in order to pass judgement on themselves. This is the strictest and most valuable, but also most important task before initiation.

Out of these considerations we get the following statements interpreting this card:

dedication to a task, a love, a belief;
knowledge of the continuation of life;
dedication to a particular issue;
the decisive transformation;
the search for one's place in the cosmos and in heaven.

The three mummies also symbolize the three soul concepts: Ka, Ba and Ach that we explained in the introduction. Going to Ka once meant dying and thus one also prayed to the Ka of the dead. Ba is the mental part of the psyche which separates from the body after death and resurrects, goes on to heaven, while Ach represents immortal power in general which is able to transfigure man and god. Here is where the seeker is initiated by recognizing the three concepts which are mutually interwoven and realizes that a person and his shadow together with Ka, Ba and Ach make up the complete individual.

The first stage of the High Priestess is also the last stage, the seventh stage, of the Way of Isis, who has now completed her work on the seeker, by the fact that she - as once with Osiris - provides those who are in transition to another world, those who are crossing the threshold, with immortal power, if these seekers believe in her and in the great divine work.

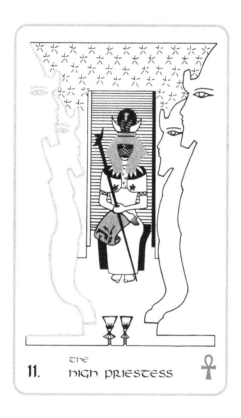

11. THE
HIGH PRIESTESS

XX. RESURRECTION

Number:

XXI

Transformation of the staff:

THE GODDESS NUT

Motto:

YOU ARE IN THE UNIVERSE - THE UNIVERSE IS EVERYTHING

XXI. THE UNIVERSE

A first glance reveals the mother of Ra the sun god, Nut, who swallows the sun every evening to birth it anew the next morning. She is depicted as a female figure with her feet at the eastern and her head at the western horizon (south is at the top). Nut is supported by the deity, Shu, so that she does not fall down onto Geb. Shu symbolizes the airy sphere separating heaven and earth. According to the divine teachings of Heliopolis, Nut was the spouse of the earth god Geb and the mother of Osiris, Isis, Nephthys and Seth. Her picture is found on lids of coffins, in books of magic and in royal tombs.

The earth, shown as a hermaphroditic being is reclining on the ground, surrounded by flowers, i.e. by nature, and is holding the heavenly instrument, here some type of harp, in one hand. Thanks to Nut heaven and earth are separated, but nevertheless united in a higher sense. Nut is said to have been procreated by Shu (air) and the lion-like goddess Tefnut (dampness). This indicates how much the Egyptians had realized that the earth was and is only capable of supporting existence at all thanks to the atmosphere (combining air and dampness). However, they thought in pictures, not as is done nowadays in scientific and soulless facts that can never approach the inner truth. Nut was "… the great one who has become the heavens…", also the goddess of the coffin lid, which closes off the deceased from those still living, as it closes off the seekers before the final initiation, since they wish to come closer to Nut - goddess of the heavens.

Nut is believed to have the power of giving new birth to a dead man or woman as a star. In the primeval state of chaos, when the earth had not yet been born, the elements thus still intermingling chaotically, no order could be established. It was the act of Shu alone, in separating heaven and earth, which then first created the delimited space where the gods on the one hand and humans on the other could act, even if the gods have the power to intervene on the earth, while humans know that they can ascend into heaven, even though they cannot enter the world of the deities themselves.

This picture then shows us the basic harmony and the basic laws which the seekers are not just able to accept as given but also to truly grasp, such that the melody of heaven can sound over the earth. Heaven and earth are separated as cosmic spheres, Shu watching over these actively, but the earth, the complement of the sky, is completely included by Nut. Her hand of blessing is always close to the earth. Thus Nut is also the mother of the sun's path through the sky, essentially also the mother of the logic of the stars that we call astrology, here shown by the golden globes on the card, stages of the sun's position across the sky. These stages are infinite even if twenty-eight are clearly shown here, as the nights of the lunar cycle. Whenever two creator gods appear as a pair, the focus is placed on an understanding of the world that is still based on a 'lunar' view of things, i.e. on the interaction of moon and sun.

Shu, who initiated the separation and also guarantees it, later also symbolized the created world, for by his separation of earth from heaven he created the basic polarity, the dualism which made the shaping and forming first possible.

After that opposites became manifest, such as those of 'heart and tongue', or 'mind and word'. 'And the word of God arose from what the heart thought and what the tongue ordered…'

Horus was the heart and Thoth the tongue. The heart thinks what it wants (the divine heart), while the tongue gives orders for all it desires. Now, at the last stage, the seventh, the god Thoth appears, whose way we shall finally have to take.

We have reached our goal. The seekers have arrived at their destination, initiation, already anticipated at the stage before. Now they have risen from their metaphorical coffins, understand the connection between heaven and earth, between god and man. We are dealing with the final, the seventh stage of the Way of Horus, as this god, having taken up man into himself in order to be able to contribute something of the divine back to man, now receives the initiated. For this act no further pictures are needed; the gods are living within us.

If we place the card of the High Priestess alongside this card XXI we can sense a close connection, made alone by the very intensively star-spangled night sky. The High Priestess was depicted as still being very reserved, however: great monuments stood guard over her; whereas the goddess Nut is so close to man here that he imagines he can reach out and touch her, indeed is allowed to touch her. The veil has fallen, the initiated have a clear view into heaven, and heaven is very close to them.

This leads us to the following interpretation factors:

being placed within an order or system;
acceptance of the order;
connection with the universe;
the achieved goal;
satisfaction or contentment;
being linked with oneself (centered) and the world (the universe).

However - even if we have taken all ways, have passed all tests and trials, even if the world of experiences may have sharpened the look inwards and outwards, and if we believe we have reached our goal - still we have not done so. We are one whole cycle nearer to the goal, maybe a decisive one; but there are many cycles ahead of us, for some of us fewer, for others more. The spiral staircase around ourselves has namely grown with us, just as challenges grow with knowledge and with understanding grows wisdom. The development never ends because the cosmos is infinite - that is without end. Therefore, we can observe ourselves once more in card XXII, the Initiate, though we certainly understand ourselves now much better.

O-XXII. THE INITIATE

We are once more on the Way. No-one is afraid of being blindfolded any longer, having once placed oneself inside the coffin of initiation. One sees - even though one believes not to see anything. Monsters always threaten one, especially those who do not set out on the way.

The goal is always the heights, however deep the way may descend, and the goal is also the depths, however steeply the way may climb upwards. The way does not only lead upwards and downwards (e.g. the daily movement of the sun), but also moves in an eternal cycle (e.g. the apparent movement of the sun north and south during the year).

As sun, moon and stars are found in an eternal cycle, but at a deeper sense cause change (for instance on the earth; and we do not know where else), so we have to apparently overcome the same Way via the cycles of experience, in order to achieve an impact which cannot perhaps be even clearly delineated. Just as the child develops to the adult and then to the aged in order to become a child once more, we also develop in cyclical fashion and yet on an ever higher, or at least different, level. This is incidentally the true secret of astrology and the tarot, which is indeed why both are immortal.

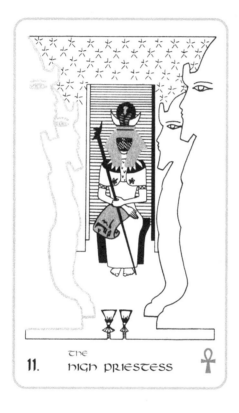

Now let us briefly review once more the three most important ways of the divine trinity:

Osiris - Isis - Horus.

THE DIVINE TRINITY AND ITS EXPECTATIONS

We have six Ways, beginning with the Initiate and returning to the Initiate. Whatever lies before or after card 0 or XXII is 'foolish', circuitous ways or detours, not ways of initiation. Before card 0 only foolishness or senselessness can be found - after card XXII the same. Whoever cannot find what he seeks in the twenty-one cards plus the Initiate's card, simply turns in a circle, in the labyrinth of his own foolishness.

This is surely one reason why cards for poker, bridge, cheap fortune-telling have developed out of the so-called Minor Arcana; cards that have basically nothing to do with the content of the Major Arcana, which only distract or promise some sort of correlations, maybe because impatience determines the attitude which does not permit everything to be found in the twenty-one cards that is to be found there.

Such things have an impact in many esoteric directions and trends. If someone somewhere - for example in astrology - does not immediately make his discoveries, new rules are set up, new fixed points appear as the latest and ultimate wisdom. The Egyptians knew this fact as did the Greeks: the true master is shown in how he sets his limits. God needed only ten rules (commandments) to maintain order in human life; instead humans created works with countless laws, works which did not bring order, which overlapped, which were exploited, and - because the sense of them was lost - were often converted to their opposite. This can be seen in every walk of life, unfortunately also on almost every esoteric or religious approach.

Yet twenty-one stages of experience are sufficient to recognize and master the three Ways under the patronage of the Divine Trinity.

The world of the gods of the ancient Egyptians was very diverse and hard to survey. We can surely assume that many myths also mixed and intermingled. It is hardly possible to distinguish the developmental paths of the gods, these paths being so labyrinthine. This provides us, however, with the task here - and we have concentrated already very much on the essential deities - of focusing our main interest on the Divine Trinity, particularly on the fact that it has proven itself so well for the souls and the knowledge of believers that other religions have in essence taken over this trinity as well in their belief system.

Each of these three deities has seven stages for their Way, both the most sacred numbers of all (three and seven) having fully confirmed their value here. It is only important to emphasize once more that these deities were always interacting with each other and are thus to be seen in totality rather than separately.

In our tarot edition the Ways of the Divine Trinity interweave. Osiris always establishes what is to be worked on, Isis deepens and Horus converts into practice. Thus all three gods - from the beginning onwards - become involved as a trinity.

What Osiris begins is ended by Horus. This should already be clear enough but it is worth repeating it once again in conclusion.

OSIRIS:

I   IV   VII   X   XIII   XVI   XIX

ISIS:

II   V   VIII   XI   XIV   XVII   XX

HORUS:

III   VI   IX   XII   XV   XVIII   XXI

THE THREE WAYS

The Way of Osiris

This way begins with the discovery of the magic powers within us, with the start, with the courage to go for initiation (card I). It continues via the laws of the pharaoh, representative of the sun, the creator of all (referring of course to Osiris) on its further course (card IV).

The next thing to learn is how to rein in one's own powers, how to steer the chariot of the god, after having mounted it, with responsibility, in order to reach the destination without harm (card VII). The fourth stage then teaches us how difficult the way we have taken in fact is, since we repeatedly have to learn to meet ourselves within our own darkness. Our task is to recognize the enigma of our own search for meaning and to solve it in order to be equipped for initiation (card X).

The encounter with the threshold, with the scorpion goddess, Serket, opens the eyes, creates awareness, for the other side of life that we call the beyond. Osiris wishes to lead us out of this world so that we grasp the great whole, the complete eternal cycle which pulses within us (card XIII).

The penultimate step is the card in which the bolt of lightening strikes, where we are then reminded not to remain inactive, not to store and save things, not to be afraid of the final consequence. The eyes of Osiris are watching over us, wherever we may be, wherever we may hide (card XVI).

The final stage is then the experience of the fullness of life, with the fortune which is to be found, and which may be worth striving for (card XIX).

This is a way of believing, comprehending, of conscious experience.

The Way of Isis

This way begins with encountering the High Priestess, since the dark side and the soul-related aspects within us need to be explored. For only the person who knows what he has within him, can know where he wants to travel to (card II).

Learning, being humble, leads us to further exploration of our soul and that causes us to kneel in front of the High Priest so that he can indicate the right way for us (card V).

The third stage of the Way of Isis: here it is a matter of weighing our conscience, questioning ourselves as to whether our own expectation is not aimed too high, whether we can continue the search (card VIII).

At the fourth stage we then encounter the power which feeds us with courage and convinces us that we can also take up the challenge against superhuman powers, if we only have confidence (card XI).

The Two Urns then remind us that the human is far from representing something 'divine', even though the divine lives and works within us (card XIV).

If this has been gratefully received, we can place trust in heavenly love and the workings of the Magic Star. Wherever the Way may lead us, the star always shines above us (card XVII).

Finally we come to the ultimate point, since we resurrect out of ourselves, since initiation takes place here, since our departure from this earth is anticipated (card XX).

It is the way of the female deity, the way of the mother, but also the way of the lovers and the true companion for life, the way of the sub-conscious, of the soul, the way of inwardness, of love, thus also the way of miracles.

The Way of Horus

This way begins with mastering life on earth, with the guidance of motherliness and the experience of subordinating oneself to the law of life at an early stage in one's life (card III).

The trial of courage in taking one's own decisions follows. When two ways of equal or similar value attract us, we should gain the insight that both ways must be travelled - even if one should be taken after the other (card VI).

The next aspect is the need to turn inwards to the self, becoming acquainted with one's own demons, the encounter with oneself in solitude and silence so that one's own true light may shine (card IX).

If this work has been completed we can place ourselves in a different position in order to observe everything from a different standpoint, as well, and to experience the opposite, thus the polarities, as a unity (card XII).

The power that is thus realized may not be abused, however, or lead to the temptation of believing one is able to do everything by oneself and does not to require the divine any longer (card XV).

If this has been understood, then the world is wide open for us and leads past places of insight and knowledge into (the mental/spiritual) heaven and to the (also inner) illumination of sun and moon (card XVIII).

This way leads the seeker to the goal, to the conclusion, as he feels 'embedded' in the order of the universe, as heavenly music sounds around him, and now released, he is able to shake off his old earthly existence (card XXI).

It is the path of reality, the way of the mind in the present, while past and future should still be recognized as serving as corner stones, as milestones.

The

Practical use

of the

Twenty-two cards

of the

Major Arcana

of the

Egyptian Tarot

There are three types of spread which are appropriate or standard procedure for this Egyptian Tarot. We really do not recommend that you bow to any querent's wish to do "fortune telling" with these cards; there are other tarot packs more suited to this. Ideally this tarot should really be concerned with orienting oneself round a standpoint, about questions such as: how do things stand for me at present? What shall I do? What are my shadow sides which I have to recognize, acknowledge and accept?

The three types of spread are:

> The Minor Egyptian Guiding Star
>
> The Major Egyptian Guiding Star
>
> The Ways of Thoth

The Minor Egyptian Guiding Star helps us to identify a temporary standpoint and orient ourselves if we have, for instance, some task ahead of us (in the sense of the timeline) which is foreseeable. This spread is mainly suitable for stress situations or for moments when we might feel we are acting beyond our capabilities, since there is maybe some external as well as internal confusion about the matter and it is a question of quickly returning to inner peace and balance.

The Major Egyptian Guiding Star, however, indicates the way for a longer period of one's life. It is really an extension of the Minor Egyptian Guiding Star; though here it is not a question of temporary events or situations, but one more concerning the basic alignment of one's own thinking and one's sub-conscious.

The Ways of Thoth spread is, so to speak, the crowning glory of the tarot and attracts us through its simplicity; indeed all three spreads are very simply structured, easy for anyone to use and to interpret. The Ways of Thoth spread reveals shadow sides which should then be acknowledged by the querent. It makes no sense to lay these cards of initiation (or to have them laid) in order then not to draw any consequences for the further course of one's life.

How should we then proceed?

With all three types of spread we lay the cards such that we can see them, that is face-up, in front of us. When doing so there is no need to place the cards in any numerical sequence. The querent then consciously lays the cards in such a way that she/he feels comfortable with them for the present moment in time. The best thing is to tell the querent: "Just place the cards in any way you feel comfortable with, such that they lie - for you personally - one after the other. You should decide the sequence yourself; the cards belong to you."

After the cards have been laid in this way the querent does not touch the cards for the time being. Then the cards should be shuffled again and from now on only used face-down. Now they are placed on the table face-down in random fashion and selected by the querent according to the instructions of the person counseling. This is done by the querent touching the cards with the fingertip and then picking them up one by one according to instructions.

Sometimes it is possible to work with cards face-up. Each person can select their own variations for handling the cards so that they 'speak' to her/him. In practice some kind of combined method has proved most successful such that a selection is made from the cards laid face-up, and then from the face-down cards. But let us go to the first type of spread, the Minor Egyptian Guiding Star, for which further information is now provided.

THE MINOR EGYPTIAN GUIDING STAR

In this spread there are two possibilities worth considering for laying the cards. From the twenty-two cards in total five are selected. In the face-up version the querent selects the first four cards, but following the instructions of the counselor.

For this version it is necessary to lay all twenty-two cards on the table face upwards. It really does not matter whether the cards are laid sequentially according to the card numbers or not. It has even proved better to lay the cards quite randomly across the surface of the table.

The person offering the counseling now asks the querent to select a card reflecting the 'problem' in which he seems to be trapped

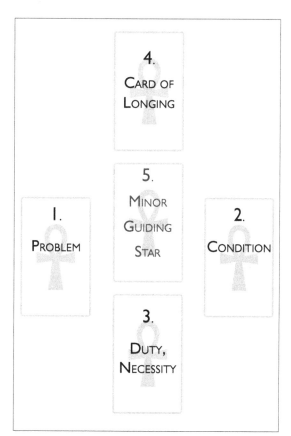

or entangled at the moment. People usually come to counseling when finding themselves in some difficult situation - unless they have come for reasons of pure curiosity. After that the 'condition', their mood, is selected, that is the card which expresses best their current state. The third card is intended to correspond to the 'necessity', or duty involved, and the fourth card, the 'longing', the desire or wish which they may have.

These cards are laid out as indicated below.

Now all the remaining eighteen cards are collected up and shuffled face-down; they should also be laid face-down on the table. The querent then chooses the fifth card face-down and places it in the middle. This gives us the Minor Egyptian Guiding Star.

Let us look at an example:

A forty-two year-old woman went to a card reader who mainly worked with the Egyptian tarot. For the card representing the problem or issue she chose number VI, 'The Two Ways'; as the inner state or condition she drew (from the face-up cards) number XX, 'Resurrection'. For the card representing duty or obligation she selected number III, 'The Pharaoh Queen', and as the card of longing or wishing she drew card number XVII, 'The Magic Star'.

The spread looked so far as shown on the opposite page, top.

The problem was to seek a second way for herself, although she was bound to the previous first way. Her wish, to free herself from 'only living for husband, family, children' in order to experience her own fulfillment, allowed her to hope for a new life. The duty of control and caring was something she felt she had grown beyond (the children had left the home) so that the longing for higher knowledge became all powerful, especially as esoteric knowledge attracted her as if by magic, like a star might. Now, without seeing the card face-up, she selected the Minor Egyptian Guiding Star. It turned out to be card number VII, 'The Chariot of Osiris'.

This led to the spread shown on the opposite page, bottom.

Interpretation: the querent is so full of inward conquering power, which may nega-

tively express itself as pride or arrogance, that she runs over the flowers of her previous life, thereby crushing them. The guiding star wants to tell her: avoid looking for your magic star externally in too stormy a fashion - that is with a too obvious new beginning - rather seek inwardly within yourself. Rein in your inward power but steer towards your destination remaining aware of your goals. When doing so it is important to avoid leaping over any stages of maturing and of acquiring esoteric knowledge. Nothing exaggerated should be undertaken! This is the message of warning which the card provides, even if the goal has been recognized and thus aimed at.

It should be emphasized that the cards should never be laid more frequently than once in two or three months. It is not good for cards to be continually selected until the result meets the expectations. If anybody tries this, they will certainly experience how the cards stop communicating anything meaningful to them. The cards will go silent, or seem confused and erratic. This is something repeatedly shown over many years of practice. The face-up selection of the Minor Egyptian Guiding Star is largely under the control of the querent. That looks quite different in the face-down version, the blindly selected version.

Here is another example from practice:

A man who had just celebrated his fiftieth birthday came for a consultation. His wife had had greater career fulfillment than he and so he approached a seminar group, which was involved with the wisdom of the occult. There he got to know and became friends with a woman fifteen years younger than himself who had fled her parental home, although she was at some time supposed to have taken over her father's business.

The man chose five cards from those spread out face-down on the table. He had done this after gathering up the cards himself, shuffling all of them and then spreading them out face-down on the table again. The selection was based on the principle that the querent pointed to the cards which were then picked up by the card reader.

The five cards were placed on top of each other. The man was then asked whether the cards should be taken from the top or bottom of the set of five. The answer came: "from the top".

As an explanation: one can assume that, if there is a preference for "from the top", the seeking is done rather by reason or the rational mind than if the preference is "from the bottom". Then people listen more to the soul, the unconscious. The five cards were laid in the following sequence (Arabic numerals).

Spread shown below.

What does the spread tell us?

The interesting thing is that the card of destruction has occurred in the position 'duty', but here this means that the man needs to find the strength to break out of his encrusted structure. It is only then that he will be able to develop his (previously) hidden magic powers.

4. CARD OF LONGING

5. MINOR STAR

1. PROBLEM

2. CONDITION

3. DUTY, NECESSITY

The card of duty and that of the problem are closely linked. His condition, however, is more related to the soul, to the High Priestess, as if he is expecting a miracle from an external source, someone who may take him by the hand. One can assume that he is looking for a new love which frees him, while in fact he alone has the duty to free himself.

Now his card of longing offers the meaning that he must free himself from everything in order to find and take his own path. For this he must first destroy his previous life. Whether he can then wait for his lady friend, that is, for his wish that she might seize the initiative, is quite uncertain. Thus his conscience has been asked whether the lady friend was nothing more than a rescuer that he had better forget.

The Minor Egyptian Guiding Star gives him a warning: overloading himself with duties and obligations just at the point when his old life has been destroyed, due to the fact that the lightning bolt of his inner wishes has struck home, is going to do him no good.

Working up from the bottom is unavoidable just as much as descending into the depths. This is his way of initiation, which requires courage and strength, but also much sacrifice of his own.

The man felt very deeply affected after that analysis and only remarked on departing: "I have to check whether I can find the strength".

THE MAJOR EGYPTIAN GUIDING STAR

While the Minor Egyptian Guiding Star is only used for situations of life arising out of the present moment, the Major Egyptian Guiding Star allows basic directions of life to be recognized.

This major guiding star is only laid according to **one** system: the first card is chosen while the cards are face-up; then the other twenty-one cards are gathered up, and the querent consulting the card reader chooses six more cards

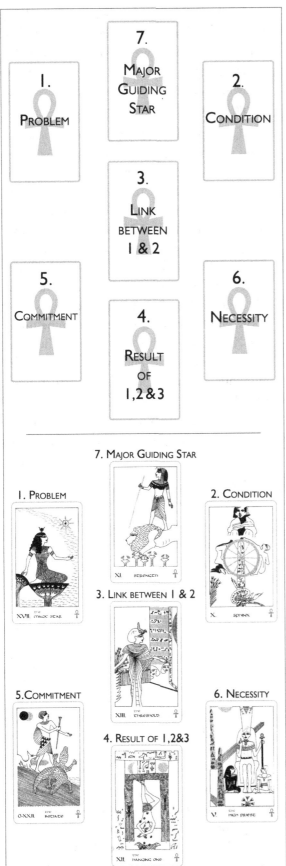

so that seven cards are used in the spread. All the other cards are put to one side. The cards are laid in the following sequence, and we will explain what each of the cards means while doing so. *(The Arabic numerals show the sequence of laying the cards and are not to be confused with the Roman numerals!)*

This means: the Problem and the Condition are linked by a card that shows how both could be combined, the Link, finally leading to the Result in card four. Card five shows the Commitment required while card six indicates the Necessity or Duties involved. Shining above all the others lies card seven, as the Guiding Star, showing the direction to follow.

An example:

A woman no longer knew how to cope with her situation. She was not very happily married. Her husband had moved out of the apartment they shared and her children hesitated as to whether they preferred to live with her or with the father. The woman showed she was very understanding about this, just relying on the belief that her love would overcome everything and that time would prove her right. Thus she chose card XVII, The Magic Star, representing Love, as card one - having total confidence in this.

The spread is presented below.

If we follow the sequence with the Arabic numerals we can easily realize what the overall situation of the woman was.

The problem says that her love has probably lost the magic of attraction, for love without inner magic becomes a strenuous condition, such as card 2 (condition), X the Sphinx, expresses. Even worse, the condition is so strenuous that love has died or has been completely transformed, has maybe even crossed the decisive threshold of having become unbearable. As a result, the only possibility remaining is to put the factor love out of one's thoughts for the present (the Hanging One) or in an esoteric sense: to transform, to turn the real things upside down, on their head, in order to gain a different viewpoint.

The commitment to be expected is the courage of freedom, even if this cannot yet be recognized in all its consequences. (The Initiate is blindfolded.) The closed or covered eyes encapsulate the challenge to recognize the blindness (also in oneself)! This leads to the necessity of submitting to tests and trials, entrusting oneself to time or even to searching for a 'teacher', a mentor for the new life to follow. Now to the Guiding Star.

Card XI, 'Strength', means that the woman has to believe in her strength, which is stronger than everything else. It should be applied with a lion's courage so that what follows can be overcome, for the strength is available to her. We recommend picking up one card after the other and interpreting each card immediately, as it is drawn, before the Major Guiding Star is revealed, in fact to analyze them in the sequence of laying them, from 1 to 7.

The Major Egyptian Guiding Star should only become visible when - thanks to the other

7. MAJOR GUIDING STAR

1. PROBLEM

2. CONDITION

3. LINK BETWEEN 1 & 2

5. COMMITMENT

6. NECESSITY

4. RESULT OF 1,2&3

cards - the problem and its potentials have been recognized. Then the Guiding Star provides the concluding element. While working through this interpretation it may well be that there is a dialog which considerably intensifies or deepens the whole interpretation.

Each picture usually generates associations which lead to insights or self-knowledge. It is of course up to every tarot consultant to individually modify the mode of laying the spreads. The important thing is that no more than seven cards are laid. In an extreme case, however, an eighth card can be drawn as a further explanation of the Egyptian Guiding Star. That was the case here. The woman did not believe that she had the strength; so she chose another card. It turned out to be number XXI, 'The Universe', which made clear that she would find her way to a new order and thus to a new place in the structure of her life.

Let us take one more look at something from our experience:

A woman who wanted to become a medical doctor was not allowed by her parents to study medicine. That is why she tried to earn her living as a non-medical practitioner or alternative healer, but that was not enough for her. In America she got to know a spiritual healer, a woman who offered to make it possible for her to get training in the field. The querent's doubts led her to the tarot counsellor.

The cards generated the spread shown opposite.

The reading ran as follows: the problem card was 'The Universe', so that leads to the question: Can I help everybody? The condition is card 2, 'The Two Urns'. A question to oneself: am I worthy to pass the test while my inner divinities observe me? (Apart from the woman being very religious, her goal was also aimed high.) The link (3) now shows that this must all be very well weighed up. The result was then card 4, XVIII, 'The Moon', which says that a long way would be required to achieve that. The commitment card shows with XX, 'Resurrection', how very much the woman was obsessed with helping other people to get on their feet again. But the necessity card warns her about not recognizing and accepting the Demon in herself. The dangers of a personal passion to help seem to be present.

What needed to be checked was whether the querent was a woman who wanted to act more from her self-interested passions and for the task she had set herself or out of a genuine inner readiness to help, which would mean that her ego would have to take second place, as is the case with every spiritual healer. So it all depended on the Major Guiding Star.

The seventh card was number III, 'The Pharaoh Queen'. This cards warns one about the need to control oneself and turn rather towards real earthly things, and thus more towards continuing the so-called usual practice of healing.

The woman was very disappointed and wanted to draw an additional card. Card IV, 'The Pharaoh', was drawn. This confirmed card III of the Major Guiding Star so that the woman now realized that the wish to become a spiritual healer was at least too early.

It is always of benefit if the querents note down the cards laid, so that they can lay them once more at home. It is then possible to meditate on these cards and even to take a look at them at various times of the day. They convey a message which will always be absorbed if the cards are intensively observed and weighed up.

This was in fact the case here. Later the woman explained that it had become clear to her that she was not yet permitted to venture too high; she was certainly not yet mature enough for that. The necessity card, 'Demon', with the cards of self-control, had clearly shown her the way that she should take.

This tarot game encourages people to reflect; it helps us to encounter ourselves. The Major Guiding Star should be accepted for a longer period of time. One can assume that the period of its 'rule' may last three years or more and that before this time has passed no further consultation should be made using this spread. So now we come to the main spread of the Egyptian tarot - namely to The Ways of Thoth.

The Ways of Thoth

In this type of spread the focus is on acceptance of the shadow, the dark side of every thing, every matter, every person, every condition. As mentioned at the start of the book, this was of the highest importance for the Egyptians, since they built their basic thinking upon day and night, upon living and dying.

The Major Arcana consists of twenty-one cards plus the card of the Initiate, giving twenty-two depictions. If we should imagine that we are in a temple where we can see eleven pictures on the one side; and then on the other side a further eleven facing them, thus each picture has its counterpart. Consequently two pictures, facing each other, always belong together. And - depending on the starting point - one picture represents a statement on the light side, the other on the dark side. Depending on which picture you start with, the picture facing always represents the shadow, the dark side, the inner complement. The whole decoration of the temple would thus depict the cycle of pictures which the seekers approach.

Picture by picture they are then studied or meditated on. It is always of importance to relate the picture pairs to each other. When the seeker concentrates on a picture, the picture then represents the light side, positive aspects, the picture at his back meanwhile expressing the dark, speaking of the hidden, that is unseen by the eyes which are directed towards the front. If the seeker turns around and looks at the picture opposite, then everything reverses; the dark has now become the light and the light has now transformed into the dark.

It is important to really get to know and remember the sequence of cards located opposite each other by noting the card names and numbers, thus allowing us to understand this cycle better. As the pairs become more familiar; you can recognize which stages of development particularly complement each other, which simply belong together.

I. The Magician..0-XXII. The Initiate

II. The High Priestess................................. XXI. The Universe

III. The Pharaoh Queen .... XX. Resurrection

IV. The Pharaoh King............................... XIX. The Sun

V. The High Priest .... XVIII. The Moon

VI. The Two Ways.................................. XVII. The Magic Star

VII. The Chariot of Osiris .... XVI. The Tower

VIII. The Scales of Conscience................................ XV. Demon

IX. The Hermit.. XIV. The Two Urns

X. Sphinx .... XIII. The Threshold

XI. Strength .... XII. The Hanging One

This provides the following list of complementary cards:

LIGHT SIDE	DARK SIDE
The Magician (I)	The Initiate (O - XXII)
The High Priestess (II)	The Universe (XXI)
The Pharaoh Queen (III)	Resurrection (XX)
The Pharaoh King (IV)	The Sun (XIX)
The High Priest (V)	The Moon (XVIII)
The Two Ways (VI)	The Magic Star (XVII)
The Chariot of Osiris (VII)	The Tower (XVI)
The Scales of Conscience (VIII)	Demon (XV)
The Hermit (IX)	The Two Urns (XIV)
Sphinx (X)	The Threshold (XIII)
Strength (XI)	The Hanging One (XII)
The Hanging One (XII)	Strength (XI)

The Threshold (XIII) .... Sphinx (X)

The Two Urns (XIV) .... The Hermit (IX)

Demon (XV) .... The Scales of Conscience (VIII)

The Tower (XVI) .... The Chariot of Osiris (VII)

The Magic Star (XVII) .... The Two Ways (VI)

The Moon (XVIII) .... The High Priest (V)

The Sun (XIX)) .... The Pharaoh King (IV)

Resurrection (XX) .... The Pharaoh Queen (III)

The Universe (XXI) .... The High Priestess (II)

The Initiate (O - XXII) .... The Magician (I)

Each light card now has its dark side, which, however, expresses nothing essentially negative. It is simply a matter of accepting the shadow side as a subconscious element that supports one, an intrinsic developmental power.

The 'Demon' may thus well represent the light, conscious factors. Whoever draws this card, also simultaneously draws 'The Scales of Conscience'. It is only cards representing light sides that are drawn. If this should be the Demon, it means that a powerful but as yet unfocused power or energy is involved, the application of which has to be weighed up precisely. Whoever draws 'The Magic Star' as being a light feature, has to consider that on the shadow side 'Two Ways' are open, or: the subconscious makes it clear that a decision needs to be made if The Magic Star is to truly shine in full glory.

Whoever draws 'The Resurrection', the revival of energies after (say) some sort of defeat, has to be aware that the shadow power warns of the need to master any everyday, earthly events and happenings which arise (The Pharaoh Queen). If 'The Hermit', say, is drawn as a light element stating that this person wishes to withdraw into himself, then the dark side is also involved; that means that happiness is not only to be found within oneself. The Hermit has to realize that the blessing of the creator also belongs to the deal. If we wish to withdraw, we should not simply shut ourselves off completely from our surroundings; we should realize that the Divine continues to guide and lead us, even if it is in an esoteric sense.

For the 'Ways of Thoth' spread we need eight cards in total; when we lay this spread, card eight (using the Arabic numerals for counting the sequence) is then 'Thoth's Advice' to us. There is only one variation of the spread and it should if possible not be modified.

The first three cards should be selected face-down. Of course they could also be selected face-up, but this causes the problem that many people who already know this tarot version or use it frequently already know the complementary card or the counterpart and thus know where their shadow sides lie.

Whoever does not know the pack and spread can select the cards face-up. After each card selected (face-up or face-down) the counsellor takes out the counterpart card and lays it alongside at an appropriate later point. The cards are then shuffled once more and the second card drawn, the counterpart being taken out by the advisor and so on.

The Spread:

Card 1		Complementary card for 1
THE SITUATION		SHADOW OF THE SITUATION
Card 2		Complementary card for 2
THE WISH		SHADOW OF THE WISH
Card 3		Complementary card for 3
THE FEAR		SHADOW OF THE FEAR
Card 4		Complementary card for 4
THE REALITY		THOTH'S ADVICE

In practice this means that the first card chosen describes the personal Situation of the querent. The complementary card explains this further. The second card drawn or chosen describes the querent's Wish which is then elucidated by the complementary card. The third card reflects the anxieties involved, the Fear, which is then illuminated by the complementary card once more. Card four will then show the overall context as the Reality, the complementary card to which is 'Thoth's advice', which should now be followed for the near future.

Three cards are selected from the newly shuffled cards placed face-down on the table at random. It helps if querents are made aware that it is their shadow, their valuable and creative dark side, which selects the cards. The querent's feeling for the cards is thus made more acute; and it is also good if the middle finger of the left hand is used to point at the cards because there is a certain serendipity, an ability to make unexpected and beneficial chance discoveries, in doing so.

The finger passes close over the cards, the querents perhaps sensing that one card sends out more warmth, another a cold feeling. It really does not matter here if such sensations are proven or not; it is exclusively a matter of the intense concentration of the querent. It is also of no importance whether the querent has previously explained her/his problem or not. The tarot counsellor should grasp the situation on the basis of the cards. Naturally a lot of practice and also experience are required here.

Once card 1 has been selected, the one showing the Situation, it is also possible for the querent to speak about this until the querent becomes fully aware of the complementary or shadow card to it. (The card reader knows - after a period of familiarity - which shadow cards belong to which light cards.) The Situation in total, however, is first really discussed with the querent taking the light and the dark cards together, before moving on to the Wish. This in turn is documented with two cards and subsequently leads by the same process to recognizing the Fear. The wish and the fear are mostly closely connected, since every wish can generate a fear or anxiety.

Just a few more points regarding the light and dark sides are provided below. These statements are, however, by no means enough for the interpretation.

I - O/XXII

The Magician has to accept that a lack of knowledge, awareness or insight is present within him

II - XXI

The High Priestess is only striving towards the Universe, but does not yet possess it

III - XX

The duties and obligations of the everyday world should not darken our view of what will follow in future

 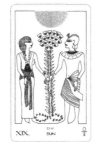

IV - XIX

Whatever dominates or rules must never shut out or suppress the sun

V - XVIII

The High Priest monitoring others has to set out on the Way as well

VI - XVII

Doubt must be overcome by love

VII - XVI

Victory may lead to destruction

VIII - XV

Without weighing things up with one's conscience
the Demon will triumph by having its way

IX - XIV

The Hermit needs the blessing of the Divine

X - XIII

No risk without daring to cross a new Threshold

XI - XII

He who stands at the peak must be ready for reversing

XII - XI

Reversing takes all one's strength

XIII - X

Crossing a new Threshold involves risk

XIV - IX

You only reach the Divine by looking into the self

XV - VIII

Our Demons must be weighed by our conscience

XVI - VII

Destruction can lead to victory

XVII - VI

Love requires making decisions

XVIII - V

The new way needs an examination of the self

XIX - IV

The power of the Sun desires mastering and placing under control

XX - III

Resurrection leads to new obligations

XXI - II

The Universe must be protected by the High Priestess

O / XXII - I

Insight into one's own lack of knowledge and understanding wakens magic powers

Example:

A scientist had got intensively involved with paranormal studies after his retirement. Before that he had radically rejected such things for sixty years, but had come upon astrology because of a dream and due to the encounter with a woman who was very interested in the subject. He was then filled with the urge to get to know all sorts of occult trends. He studied them with an almost scientific meticulousness and was suddenly confronted with the question as to whether he should consider undergoing a reincarnation therapy.

His wife warned him about such a real adventure of the soul, particularly as there is no guarantee about the quality of the therapists and thus any person doing such a reincarnation experiment. That is when he asked a tarot counsellor.

The first card drawn was The Pharaoh King, describing the Situation:

The scientist understood this as a definite 'yes', but the counsellor expressed his opinion as follows: 'this looks more like a 'no' to me since the card is in fact stating that you should exercise self-control, i.e. you ought not to carry out everything that you want to do; and the shadow seems basically to be saying that you should remain in your 'light' world.'

CARD 1

IV. PHARAOH KING

LIGHT SIDE SITUATION

COMPLEMENT

XIX. SUN

SHADOW SITUATION

CARD 2

XIII. THRESHOLD

LIGHT SIDE WISH

COMPLEMENT

X. SPHINX

SHADOW WISH

CARD 3

XX. RESURRECTION

LIGHT SIDE FEAR

COMPLEMENT

III. PHARAOH QUEEN

SHADOW FEAR

CARD 4

XV. DEMON

REALITY

COMPLEMENT

VIII. THE SCALES OF CONSCIENCE

THOTH'S ADVICE

Everyone who undertakes reincarnation work and does regression under hypnosis has to be clear about the fact: the experience is impossible to forget.

However, the next card drawn was meant to correspond to the true Wish - that is the soul's wish. The man searched over the cards now much more slowly and more carefully.

The wish was clear. The Threshold revealed that the man had the powerful wish to step back in time from this world and into another world. But the dark shadow side clearly indicates that it would be difficult subsequently to find his way back to the light side.

The man thus received the warning when he chose the third card face-down which reflected his inner fears.

The Resurrection emerged as the Fear card. This indicates that the querent was really not quite sure as to whether a true regression would be successful, even if he should really long for it.

The shadow was revealed in card III, The Pharaoh Queen. The man was asked what his wife would say to all of this. His reply: 'I think she is afraid that it will become more difficult in our marriage'. He had wanted to say 'still more difficult' but corrected it at the last moment.

Now it was a question of what the fourth card, Reality, would show. It turned out to be card XV, Demon, with its shadow card, The Scales of Conscience.

He is obsessed by a really hazardous wish that is driving him onwards and has taken hold on him to some extent, a wish that should be well considered!! Thoth's advice confirms this, for the Scales of Conscience does not say 'no' but rather warns that he should do a very intensive self-review.

It is well worth reviewing the spread opposite as a whole

Now one can ponder a bit more deeply on the overall picture and then it becomes evident that the wish for the Shadow quite strongly dominates the light side, the conscious thinking. The Shadow cards, however, definitely give a warning and Thoth's advice is quite clear.

This advice is always the only decisive factor, by the way. Even if everything up to then has indicated that the question would apparently have a positive answer, Thoth's advice can turn everything around. This is naturally true for the reverse situation. If everything appears to be so-called negative, Thoth's advice can guide everything into a positive direction.

Why do we then draw the previous cards? That was a question repeatedly asked in seminars. The answer is that in doing so there is a process of intimate self-questioning involved. Otherwise we could just express a wish and draw a card. But this way of treating the matter will hardly lead us and any querents onto the right path. That is why this spread includes eight cards. The eight is incidentally the number of the lemniscate, the highest number in the sense of significance, the very number of Isis.

As with the Major Egyptian Guiding Star, that is intended to show the way ahead for a longer time period, it is a good thing to do some meditating about this final card from Thoth's spread. It would also be a good thing for a querent to place Thoth's card, i.e. the advice card, somewhere in his/her home so that he or she can catch sight of it from time to time.

Let us turn to one more example:

A young man came for a consultation; he made an intelligent but rather helpless impression. He tended - according to what he said - to be rather adventurous, wanted to travel out into the world, to India and Egypt. However, his parents saw him alone as the administrator, guardian and shaper of their inheritance, a rather large company. In fact the whole matter had already been decided, since the young man had never been able to break free from his upbringing. So he submitted to his parents. But there must have been some permanent revolutionary dwelling in his soul since something in him kept rebelling. That is how it came to the tarot reading.

As the Situation he chose The Pharaoh Queen from the face-up cards.

The situation showed the domination, the submission to the system, to the practical administrative tasks. But in the dark-side there is a permanent slumbering wish to escape from this, to resurrect as if newly transformed in order to be able to start something fresh.

CARD 1	COMPLEMENT	CARD 2	COMPLEMENT

LIGHT SIDE SITUATION	SHADOW SITUATION	LIGHT SIDE WISH	SHADOW WISH

CARD 3	COMPLEMENT		CARD 4	COMPLEMENT

LIGHT SIDE FEAR	SHADOW SITUATION		REALITY	THOTH'S ADVICE

The Wish card was selected:

The wish to turn everything on its head is strongly anchored in his consciousness and in the dark-side strength is added to that consciousness. He can tame the lion, that means in this case the parental authority. But what is he afraid of?

Answer: he is afraid of the trials to be faced, does not want to be the prodigal son who has to return, does not wish to do more that he can cope with. And in the dark-side this also doubtless means that the new adventurous life in other parts of the world would perhaps only attract him for a short time. Now the fourth card was to decide.

In reality this young man is inwardly a seeker, a blind person with a risk of slipping over the edge. Thoth's advice then goes in the direction of the querent first having to develop his magic powers, learning to handle them, and standing only at the very beginning of a possible new way!

The person concerned was not very enthusiastic about that, but also not discouraged. He put pressure on his parents until they gave him three months vacation so that he could have a look at his India, his Egypt.

From Cairo the young man wrote that he had joined an archaeological group in Thebes and that he would need a longer period to establish clarity about his future way. This hit the parents like a shock, but what could they do? After two years they accepted the decision of their eldest son and transferred everything to his younger brother, having first disinherited the eldest son of everything but an obligatory share.

For further meditation we have the whole picture on the following page.

Whoever feels his way into this eight-card spread will recognize that all the cards have been selected in a sequence that makes sense in itself. The mother rules the situation; the young man wishes to be reborn and begin completely anew, his soul trusting that he has the strength to do so. But he stands before the testing of his conscience, whether he is ready to set off on his own quite personal and arduous path through life.

CARD I
Light-Side Situation

III.
THE PHARAOH QUEEN

COMPLEMENT
Shadow Situation

XX.
RESURRECTION

CARD 2
Light-Side Wish

XII.
THE HANGING ONE

COMPLEMENT
Shadow Wish

XI.
STRENGTH

CARD 3
Light-Side Fear

V.
THE HIGH PRIEST

COMPLEMENT
Shadow Fear

XVIII.
THE MOON

CARD 4
Reality

0 - XXII.
THE INITIATE

COMPLEMENT
Thoth's Advice

I.
THE MAGICIAN

Afterword

We have travelled a long way. It is a way which has led us millennia back to the cradle of western civilization - to Egypt. But it is also a way back into ourselves, for who does not deeply long to experience something of the sense of initiation? A person will often feel very small and insignificant there, but he will recognize all the more clearly the gifts that the blessing of the gods allow him to receive. The gods live within us, even if we mostly project them into the heavens. The Egyptians still lived close to their gods, lived in or near the temple; thus they were all aware of the initiation ceremonies.

The tarot is perhaps not the oldest book we know, but it is certainly the one with the deepest esoteric insight, and without doubt thus the wisest book that exists, if we leave aside the books of religion.

Whoever has gone ahead on the way of initiation, may perhaps stand still for a while, but something will drive him onwards until he has taken all the twenty-one stages of the Way (even if not in numerical sequence). A way that fulfills the soul and creates knowledge, that expands the view and helps to distinguish important from unimportant.

These tarot pictures open doors which would otherwise remain shut. Thus you can call them a secret code. However, it can be used only by those who have as-similated the pictures and have really understood them. The tarot may even help us under certain circumstances to discover the sense in life, even if the way is the goal.